THE BLUE BOX

Three Lives in Letters

———

Sallie Bingham

Sarabande  Books

LOUISVILLE, KENTUCKY

Managing Editor
Sarabande Books, Inc.
2234 Dundee Road, Suite 200
Louisville, KY 40205

Library of Congress Cataloging in Publication Data

Bingham, Sallie.
The blue box : three lives in letters / by Sallie Bingham. — First edition.
    pages cm
Summary: "This family history centered around three women from three generations
spans the Civil War through the Jazz Age. Fans of Sallie Bingham's work will especially
appreciate her parents Mary and Barry's romance that unfolds in letters and finally results
in marriage. Bingham beautifully demonstrates an inheritance of emotion, morality,
ideology, and most lasting of all, irreverence."—Provided by publisher.
    ISBN 978-1-936747-78-8 (paperback : acid-free paper)
    1. Bingham, Sallie—Family. 2. LeFroy, Sallie Montague, 1850–1942. 3. Caperton,
Helena Lefroy, 1878–1962. 4. Bingham, Mary Caperton, 1904– 5. Mothers and
daughters—United States. 6. Intergenerational relations—United States. 7. Women
authors, American—Biography. 8. Women—United States—Biography. 9. Wom-
en—United States—Correspondence. 10. American letters. I. Title.
    PS3552.I5Z48 2014
    818'.5403—dc23
    [B]
                                    2013048733

Cover and interior layout by Kirkby Gann Tittle.

Manufactured in Canada.

This book is printed on acid-free paper.

Sarabande Books is a nonprofit literary organization.

The Kentucky Arts Council, the state arts agency, supports Sarabande
Books with state tax dollars and federal funding from the National
Endowment for the Arts.

FOR

Sallie Montague Lefroy
Helena Lefroy Caperton
Mary Caperton Bingham

MY FOREMOTHERS

The growing good of the world is partly dependent on unhistoric acts; and that things are not so ill with you and me as they might have been, is half owing to the number who lived faithfully a hidden life, and rest in unvisited tombs.

—George Eliot, *Middlemarch*

INTRODUCTION

All three were tiny women.

Sallie, Helena, and Mary—my great-grandmother, my grand-mother and my mother—barely topped five feet. In girlhood, they were as proud of their small waists as of their intelligence, which was considerable. Writing was their blessing, and each used it to create a reality more appropriate to her personality, more manageable, and more forgiving of her time.

Autumn Garner, Sallie called her gilded memoir, written for her granddaughters in the 1940s, toward the end of her long life.

Legends of Virginia, Helena named her second collection of short stories, published in 1950, with its light dressing of sarcasm.

Mary forged a romantic legend from the many courtship letters that documented her four-year pursuit of the man who would later become my father.

All three women were tiny, but they held their heads high, though their pride was based in part on an unexamined faith, never directly spoken, in their racial superiority. The accoutrements of gentility defined them, as well as an adherence to a written and spoken language shaped by nineteenth-century English fiction and poetry, classical Greek and Latin texts, and the King James Bible.

Through the devastation of the Civil War, financial disaster, and the early loss of her husband, Sallie turned to pen and paper to record a version of her life that must have been to her, at times, more palatable than the reality itself.

For Helena, the language of Edwardian romance, already outdated, sugared the tales of her struggles in raising six daughters and provided a bulwark against the chaos that her large family and lack of money brought to her door.

Mary's education—she was the first in her family to graduate from college—gave her a larger vocabulary, based on those classical texts and her family's ever-dependable King James Bible, slightly influenced but never overwhelmed by the radical changes of the 1920s.

Long before I knew the details of my foremothers' lives, I recognized the theme that ran like a steel thread through their disparate personalities: indomitability, even when the times called for suppleness. To what extent did this steel thread tie up their secrets? How closely linked were their unquestioned feelings of superiority—social, racial, moral, intellectual—to their ability to survive, even flourish, as their fortunes sank and rose?

For years, I could only speculate.

Then, one spring day in 2011, my sister Eleanor was sorting the house after our mother's death and found a large blue box on the top shelf of Mary's closet. "It's full of things," she told me: folded and refolded letters, a few labeled with a distant relation's curatorial notes; an old prayer book; worn college bluebooks; faded manuscripts and deeply creased articles—all earthly remains of Sallie, Helena, and Mary.

Eleanor joked, "I was about to put it all in the dumpster" along with a lifetime of trash. A regard for the past prevented her; our niece Emily concurred, knowing the value of those "things" that remain. Jointly, they decided to loan the blue box to me.

As Emily handed it over, I felt excitement fired by an element of dread.

As it does so often, the official record belongs to the men in the family, who in our case made speeches and were quoted in newspaper stories. This blue box contained the women's stories, which always disturb, however unintentionally, the official record.

I studied the box as I held it awkwardly in my arms—its hue neither azure nor turquoise, but a soft cornflower blue.

Measuring 20" by 16" by 5", the box was definitely too large for casual storage. It had to hold more than the detritus of scraps, yarn, snapshots, old buttons, and canceled checks that usually ends up in a shoebox in a woman's closet.

The box seemed designed for some mysterious purpose, although it had rested undisturbed for decades. For decades, no one who had been aware of it had cared to look inside. Finally, I lifted the lid and peered in.

I saw nests of papers: a marriage certificate listing eighteen slaves by name, the property of my great-great-grandmother; Civil War correspondence between two brothers, one of whom died, nearly starving and half mad as the consequence of a head wound, shortly after the war ended; tightly folded introductions to long-forgotten speakers at a Richmond women's club. These were Sallie's.

Next came Helena's manuscripts, the accumulation of her attempts to become a professional writer: humorous personal essays and strange, often disturbing, short stories that sometimes made it to publication.

Finally, I found the record of Mary's college career, and the courtship letters that led, after four excruciating years, to her marriage with my father.

Although they were not in the box, I remembered photographs: Sallie, at her debut in white lace and flowers and a delighted smile, and at ninety, proudly bearing the distinction of being "the oldest living debutante"; Helena, trussed in satin on her wedding day; Mary, prim on a lawn in cardigan, skirt, and lace-collared blouse.

And I thought: tiny, yes, but indomitable.

I took the box home.

Later, as I sifted through its contents, the spidery string holding together the old prayer book frayed, and the dainty red-and-white thread around reticule-sized essays unraveled. The blue covers of college examination books eighty years old separated and hung by a single staple; envelopes, originally torn open in haste, revealed ragged edges; small yellowed pages were covered with clear, well-formed handwriting, the ink still bright; and dropped keys on a 1920s typewriter had marred carefully composed English papers.

I heard, behind these sentences, languorous Virginia drawls and cultivated Anglo-Irish tones, and finally the curious mixture of these that would become the voices of my Kentucky childhood.

I am taller than these women were, or would have wanted to be, and my life has provided me with many options they could not have imagined. In many ways I live in a world they could never understand. Yet the one trait that links us is a certain unyielding resilience.

Would the blue box reveal the source of this singular trait?

Later, my sister handed me the grocery list she'd found in our mother's purse on the night she died while giving a speech. Elegantly coiffed and unfaltering, Mary was lecturing, as she had so often before, on the infinite value of words, this time in the name of a library she was urging her listeners to support.

"Grapefruit," her shopping list began, and I remembered the meager breakfast she always ate in bed, her bowl balanced on a flowered tray;

"Whipping cream," her favorite indulgence, thick enough in a Mason jar to hold up a spoon;

"Cooking oil, very thin white bread":

"Chicken" was followed by a question mark, but "bacon" was a certainty.

"Prune soufflé with whipped cream" rounded out the menu from her final grocery list.

Indulgence and self-discipline. A determination to insist on the world as desired, no need for justification, no matter the cost. The blue box, summed up in a last shopping list—or perhaps not so tidy. Nothing, as we know, is as complicated as the past.

ONE

Years ago, when I began to wonder about Sallie Montague Lefroy, my great-grandmother and namesake, I had only her memoir, *Autumn Garner*, for reference. Composed toward the end of her long life and carefully typed by my mother, this cheerful memoir revealed itself to be only a limited way to understand a complex woman. Her reflections are bound by the stereotypes of her time and censored for fear of upsetting her six granddaughters, for whom the memoir was written. Later I learned more, as I delved deep into the contents of the blue box, which contained letters, essays, and speeches Sallie wrote while she was living the life she commemorated in her memoir.

Autumn Garner opens with a description of Sallie's childhood in the decades before and during the Civil War, or the War, as she certainly called it.

She was born in 1850 into the highly regarded Montague family of Richmond, Virginia, and thoroughly enjoyed her life as a privileged family's beloved daughter in the antebellum South both in Richmond proper and on the more remote family plantations before the Union victory in 1865.

As a young child in the 1850s, Sallie would have overheard heated discussions of the Fugitive Slave Act, the Kansas-Nebraska Act, and the Dred Scott decision, all of which aggravated tensions between the slave-holding South and the increasingly industrialized North. While Virginia, a border state and the birthplace of four U.S. presidents, did not initially align itself with the Confederacy, after the 1861

Confederate firing on Fort Sumter even moderate Virginians were drawn into the fierce oncoming conflict.

John Henry Montague and Melinda Meredith Fox, Sallie's parents, owned two plantations outside of Richmond, as well as a house on Franklin Street, and depended on slaves to run them; there was never any question where their sympathies lay. Their roots were in the slave-holding South and those roots ran deep.

On the Montague side, the first to arrive in the New World had been "Our Pioneer Ancestor," as a plaque erected by the family in 1903 proclaims: this was Peter Montague, a servant indentured at twenty-one to Sir Francis Wyatt. Peter disembarked from Wyatt's ship, the *Charles*, at Jamestown, Virginia, in October 1621.

Peter had entered into a contract of indenture to pay for his voyage, which would otherwise have cost him half a year's wages, assuming he was employed. He was listed on the ship's manifest under the category "servant's," a list written long before the standardization of the apostrophe and its usage. At the end of his indenture Peter came into possession of a large piece of land, thanks to the Virginia Law of Freedom Due. He loomed large in his descendents' imaginations.

Sallie and her daughter, my grandmother Helena, held tightly to the claim that his ship was the first to reach the New World. Since the Plymouth Rock settlers arrived in 1620, this claim is difficult to support, and seems to depend on a need to place Peter Montague at the forefront of the New World settlers. It sometimes seems that Sallie and her descendants firmly believed the Montagues were actually the First Americans since, with the one exception of Pocahontas, they did not even pretend to acknowledge the earlier presence of the Native Americans.

Sallie was the eldest of the six children of John Henry and Melinda, closest in temperament to her only sister, Helen. Sallie was born in 1850; Beverly shortly after; Meredith in 1856; Helen in 1858; John Henry, or Johnny, in 1860; and Percy at some time before or after.

Little is preserved of Johnny and Meredith's lives other than handsome portraits, but Beverly is not pictured or mentioned in *Autumn Garner* until Sallie describes their mother's will, written in 1910. Nor is Percy mentioned, who died in 1902 and is buried in the family plot in Hollywood Cemetery, in Richmond, with his brothers and sisters.

118 Franklin Street, Richmond, VA
The Montague Home, 1869

The Montague house stood at 118 East Franklin Street, a handsome three-story townhouse in the area called Linden Row. Bought by Sallie's father in 1863, the house signaled the family's impressive recovery from the financial disruptions of the War.

John Henry Senior did not serve in the War, perhaps because of his age, an eye ailment, or because he was the owner of more than twenty slaves—all causes for exemption at various points during the conflict. But his absence from the ranks must have caused comment in Richmond during a period when eight hundred thousand Southerners of military age served, two-thirds of those eligible.

Further aggravating the problem of his civilian status, John Henry prospered during the war; as early as December 1866, he was credited with the proceeds from the sale of 115 bales of cotton, about 5,175 pounds, totaling $22,161.11. He was at that point president of a Richmond bank and of a large mercantile company.

Long before the war, the family's prosperity was well established. Their properties included Cherry Grove, the Montagues' plantation, as well as Green Springs in Louisa County, a Fox family inheritance; this plantation had been sold to Sallie's great-grandfather Joseph Fox in 1735—400 acres for 40 shillings. Handsome Melinda Fox Montague brought a frequently reused first name (often spelled Malinda) into the family along with the Green Springs property, as well as her connection with her great-uncle, Charles James Fox. This well-known Whig who served in the British Parliament for 38 years had been an outspoken opponent of slavery, which would have horrified his Virginia relations—perhaps the reason he was erased from the tribe's memory by the time of Sallie's writing.

The two plantations and the townhouse in Richmond provide the backdrop for Sallie's memoir. The word "slavery" is never mentioned; the word she uses is "servants." Certainly she had heard of Lumpkin's Slave Jail in Shockoe Bottom by the James River, a holding pen for thousands of African-Americans waiting to be sold. Locals called it "Devil's Half-Acre," where many died of abuse and disease. From 1808, as many as 300,000 slaves were bought and sold in Richmond, literally "shipped down the river" to the plantations in the deep South.

And Sallie could hardly have been unaware of the Bread Riots in 1863, when Richmond was on the verge of famine and upwards of a thousand women, and some men, stormed shops and warehouses for food and were chased by troops down Franklin Street. While the rich could always acquire virtually anything, the blockade of southern ports and the Union domination of rail lines meant that "starvation parties," where no food was served, had become regular occurrences in Richmond.

While the rioting women were described by the men of Richmond's elite as "Irish and Yankee hags and harlots," some of the Montague neighbors may have given starvation parties, which might have led thirteen-year-old Sallie to question her family's comparative comfort, though no mention of any such questions exists in Sallie's letters or reminiscences.

Sallie's mother would certainly never have countenanced any questioning of the system on which their society depended. Since none of Melinda's letters were kept, she is to some degree a cipher in my story. But according to family legend and a few surviving photographs, her marriage in 1848 seems to have been full of affection; it lasted for sixty years, commemorated by an extraordinary photograph taken in 1908.

In the photograph, John and Melinda, both in their eighties, sit side by side in a dusky parlor, backed by a wall of family portraits; Melinda wears a lace jabot and cap, her severely elegant profile suggesting authority and an ageless beauty. John has pasted a flange of dark hair

Sixtieth Anniversary portrait of John Henry Montague and
Melinda Fox Montague, with Mary Jefferson, 1908

Note written by Helena Trench Lefroy Caperton

over his bald spot; he wears a starched wing collar and spats and stares off at an angle.

Between and behind them, a middle-aged African-American woman in white apron and cap looks directly at the camera with an ambiguous smile; she is labeled "Mary Jefferson, long the faithful attendant of the latter."

An unquestioning belief in the faithfulness of slaves and former slaves formed Sallie's thinking. "In the early days, our servants in the South 'belonged,'" she explains in her memoir, "and when my generation began my grandmother Melinda Fox made Mammy Polly a welcome present to my parents."

Sallie describes her place in the household: "Mammy Polly reigned in our nursery and commanded her subordinate helpers until the day of her death.

"She could shell peas and preach simultaneously," Sallie writes. "Waiting for you, Miss, waiting for you," Polly warned when Helena found a worm in her garden.

Polly was kept busy supervising the six Montague children, especially during the summers when Melinda and her brood decamped to Green Springs, leaving John Henry in Richmond.

During the summer of 1851, John Henry writes his wife:

> I return to this, to me, most delightful employment, a chat with you through the mails, but how inferior is it to the face to face or rather side by side converse we shall hold on Monday next. My heart bounds at the thought that I shall see your dear face so soon & look once more at those little ones who I hope hereafter will reflect your virtues as they now do your image. Do not point them to me when you are ready to train them up for future usefulness, for I am conscious of too many imperfections but be yourself their Model and bright exemplar in after times.... In the lively, charming accomplished little Sally I recognize a "pocket edition" of you; bless her little heart, how I long to have her in my arms again, and Beverly, that poor fellow who has so manfully withstood the "battle and the breeze," the ship wreak and the storm, and yet lives to laugh at the buffetings of the jealous fates who 'twould seem have been striving to thwart his brilliant destiny. Don't you observe sometimes on his thoughtful countenance the play of ideas that he has not yet the power to express? I have often fancied that I could. This may be a mere idea of my own, born of love and hope, and a sealed volume to others, but WE may surely compare notes on the subject with each other. Why what would we care what the unappreciative world shall say? Have I dwelt too long on this subject?

His question hinted at Melinda's pain; there was something wrong with Beverly. Melinda's will, leaving the income of her estate to Beverly in trust, indicated that he was not expected as an adult to be able to take care of himself; he outlived her by only one year.

There would have been little discussion of Beverly's handicap, whatever it might have been. Later, Johnny became a heavy drinker, but that, too, would have been passed over in silence.

Apart from the numerous servants—all slaves—dedicated to their comfort, the Montague children were left very much on their own. Like her brothers and sister, Sallie was introduced early to this system of parental "benign neglect," which her daughter Helena and her granddaughter Mary would champion.

Outbursts of emotion were always deemed inappropriate, as, Sallie recounts in her memoir, when she screamed with terror on overhearing a slave woman having a seizure in the night.

"Such nonsense," she was told, "to be frightened by such a poor thing." Sallie adds, "Children were not permitted nerves in those hardy old days." There is, tellingly, no mention of what happened to the person who had the seizure, or even her name.

Sallie mentions her sister affectionately, but with few details. Helen would be commemorated after her death in 1911 for her seven years as treasurer of the Richmond Woman's Club, especially her "neat and well nigh perfect records," as well as her "exquisite refinement" and her "confident and serene faith . . . some of her verses deserve to live, whether or not capricious fortune preserves them." Capricious fortune did not. She never married.

Sallie's younger brother, Meredith, a handsome rake in later photographs, inspired another anecdote: fooling around with a gun, he shot the family's cook. Sallie relates this with delight: "Meredith shot the cook!" Sallie limits her report to what appears to her to be the only consequence: the buckshot was picked out of the woman's back and life went on. Again, for Sallie, there was no question of interrogating the social order that surrounded her. This order supported her family, and, as with young Sallie's nighttime alarm or Beverly's mysterious incapacity, anything that upset order in their world must not be acknowledged.

For this family, even physical pain was expected to be overlooked whenever possible. While swimming in the James River at a particularly dangerous spot, Meredith broke his ribs on rocks but, in line with the family code of behavior, never told his parents.

Sallie's mother Melinda rarely appears in the memoir, but when she does, she is the ubiquitous Victorian icon, the Angel in the House, lightly springing from her four-poster bed to attend to slaves or children taken ill in the night.

Melinda's other duty was preparing Cherry Grove for the family's long summer visit. At the plantation, the African-American children provided companionship for the white children. "We did not choose our servitors," Sallie writes, "they chose us to command. 'I gwine to belong to Miss Sallie,'" she claims one of the slave girls proclaimed while others picked Helen. The boys, she asserts, naturally preferred the brothers. Even as children, Sallie and her siblings were already convinced that these people, precisely because they were not of her family's race, were happy to serve those who treated them as property.

Sallie describes in her memoir how, in the same vein, horses and mules were available to ride "generally with some kindly guide to instruct. We never had saddles till we could stick on bareback."

•

Sallie's experience of the Civil War, which broke out when she was eleven, was distinct from other Southern girls' because her father did not enlist, and her brothers were too young to serve. The war did not immediately impinge on her family's daily life.

Even so, some of the worst slaughter of the war took place within sight and sound of Richmond, which was the Confederate capital. The stench of unburied corpses from the disastrous Wilderness Campaign of 1864 suffused the streets. Citizens pressed handkerchiefs soaked in peppermint oil to their noses, but Sallie in her memoir never mentions the smell, or any awareness of nearby deaths, only that, once the war began, everyone had to get used to the almost perpetual booming of cannon.

When her father turned the Richmond house into a military hospital, Sallie's account is almost lyrical: "Every room was filled with beds and soldiers, and Mothers came from far away places in the South to nurse their boys. The Mothers were so kind," one of them inviting Sallie to bring her dolls and play on her son's bed. "I was so glad that he was getting well. He seemed so merry and amused, and I was glad his leg had stopped hurting."

Her imagination provided escape. During these war years, Sallie became the self-described "well-accredited Story-Teller of the juvenile circle. Fairy tales and wonder stories were my delight, so much so that our Mother found it wise to limit my reading of such fiction to two stories a day."

To counter these flights of fancy, Melinda instituted a two-hour reading session in history or the classics, which Sallie thoroughly enjoyed. The only title she mentions is William H. Prescott's 1843 *History of the Conquest of Mexico*, an account as bloodthirsty as any Grimms' tale. "Even the cruelties of Prescott's 'Conquests' were not allowed to deter me," Sallie writes.

As the war dragged on, its deprivations were felt in Richmond, eventually blockaded by Union forces. Perhaps the Montagues were supplied with vegetables, chickens, and fruit from Cherry Grove, which lay inside the lines, sparing them the hunger that haunted the rest of the city.

Though in her memoir she doesn't mention food deprivation, Sallie recalls that, at twelve years old, she bemoaned her lack of toys and new clothes. Her "cherished family of china dolls looked more and more as if they too had been in battle." After seeing a doll for sale, a "staring black-eyed beauty in a shop on Broad Street," Sallie flew home to ask her father for forty dollars (in devalued Confederate money); he, ever indulgent, gave her the large sum and she bought the doll, although she reports that Polly tried to shame her out of it.

Once Richmond was besieged, "one could get no new clothes." Sallie and her sister made do with one cotton dress each. She describes how they obtained these dresses:

> The cotton was grown on the plantation, it was spun into thread by Aunt Sarah in her cabin and woven into black and white checks by a neighbor who had a loom. But the real and choice triumph of these rare costumes was the trimming: pink skirt braids plaited and outlining the shoulders, necks and wrists.

Skirt braid was the coarse braid once used under long dresses to lift them up and protect their hems from dust.

A little later, Sallie was excited by the news that a ship had run the blockade, bringing medicine for the wounded soldiers thronging into Richmond as well as "a bolt of the fine woolen stuff called merino. . . . So lovely it was to our eyes that we could hardly keep from stroking it." New dresses were soon made for the sisters.

Only one further incident from the late days of the War merited inclusion in Sallie's memoir.

"Our dear Mother usually made a short visit to the plantation in the early spring before moving the family for the summer," she writes. While Melinda was at the plantation on April 2, 1865, President Davis and his cabinet fled Richmond, and the retreating Confederate troops prepared to burn the tobacco warehouses and armament depots along the James River to prevent them from falling into Union hands.

Nevertheless, though all rail lines and roads out of the city were blocked, Sallie's father sent word somehow to Melinda urging her to return, a curious request that would bring her and her young son into the heart of danger.

Sallie's mother started out to return that night with little Johnny, driven by David, the coachman. They began to pass Confederate soldiers retreating from the city who called out in the darkness, "You going the wrong way, lady, better turn and go along with us." But Melinda Fox Montague pressed on.

When they reached the last intact bridge into the city, David saw men on the far side "with blazing torches . . . firing the worn timbers" to prevent the invading Union soldiers from crossing.

According to Sallie's memoir, David said, "What shall I do, Mistress? Wherever you want to go I will drive you." Melinda responded "in a quiet, firm voice, 'Drive on,'" and the horses "with a bound and a rush carried their most precious burden . . . safely across the burning bridge."

Melinda arrived at home to hear "a deafening roar" that rattled the windows: the powder magazine near the river had been blown up. Then news came that "the lower end of the town was on fire. All of Main Street was in ruins. Nothing could be rescued. My father's office shared the fate." In his safe, the set of turquoise jewelry sent from England by Melinda's relative, Charles James Fox, melted into a molten mass.

How David was able to drive the horses through fire that ultimately consumed over half the city is the miracle of the story. Sallie explains it by noting that he had taken care of the horses for years and they responded to his voice.

During the years following the war, Sallie learned the lesson that would mold her memoir:

> I knew later how wonderful it was that our dear parents kept the
> distress and anxiety of those hard days from clouding our young

lives. There was financial ruin, hopes blasted, and a country disenfranchised and overrun by the very scum of the earth from the North.

Sallie described the changes brought by the Emancipation Proclamation with her usual deference to the pervasive myth that would keep racism and its attendant evils alive in the South—the myth that African-Americans had both deserved and enjoyed their servitude and that they wanted nothing more than to continue as they had before. According to her account, the family's freed slaves turned to their former master and mistress for advice, and remained, gladly, in servitude, cared for solicitously the rest of their lives.

By the time she wrote her memoir, she must have known that many former slaves, especially the young and able-bodied, fled the plantations, but the myth of their preference for lifelong care as a reward for lifelong peonage was too fundamental to her to understand otherwise.

Questioning received wisdom was not part of Sallie's education. Though her first teacher was so young she would later teach Sallie's granddaughter, Sallie's main education occurred at a school run by Dr. D. Lee Powell. There, she followed "a more advanced curriculum" than what she'd had, including science and math. More important, Sallie began to hear "from our elders and instructors . . . to prepare for a life of unlooked-for vicissitude, a life different in temporal ways from that of our parents."

A blast of fresh air was stirring the old shibboleths concerning a woman's role in the newly evolving Southern economy. Sallie writes,

> Mr. Powell used to say that as he had seen Southern women reduced to poverty, he intended to teach his girls just as he would if they were boys; he had confidence in their ability, and would prepare them to gain, if necessary, a livelihood in the higher walks of life,

Sallie Watson Montague, 1877; daughter of John Henry and Melinda Fox Montague

presumably as teachers, nurses, and governesses—at the time the only occupations open to women.

A mischievous spirit, encouraged by her father, who was "somewhat blind to my indiscretions," occasionally thwarted Sallie's impulses toward conformity. Warned that her sister Helen "would be a very good child but for your influence," Sallie describes as an example the two little girls cutting illustrations from Boydell's Shakespeare, being "too young to appreciate their artistic value." They decorated the living room chairs and tables with the paper dolls.

When their father appeared, the two girls ran "as usual to see who could get the first kiss," but

> his usual sympathetic interest in what we were doing was strangely lacking. He quietly left the room. I passionately threw the foolish paper dolls aside and burst into tears. I had seen a look on my father's face and knew I had hurt him. My very dear father!

Years later, an aunt recalled John Henry Montague saying the two little girls "were so innocently happy and there was no remedy." He did not punish or even reprimand them. There was no need. Sallie's sensitivity to her father's reaction, or even to his lack of reaction, assured that her "iconoclastic ventures" would be few. The most effective discipline depended on her exquisitely overdeveloped desire to please.

Sallie's nurse, Polly, was neither as indulgent as Sallie's father, nor as effective. Polly's discipline usually involved threats of hellfire and her Biblical quotations were "superabundant."

"Being rather pert," Sallie writes, "I would sometimes indulge in reprehensible back talk," including claims that "such and such a thing was not in the Bible. Mama says it isn't," to which Polly would reply, "Go way from here, chile, if it ain't, it ought to be."

In 1863 when Sallie was thirteen, President Lincoln issued the Emancipation Proclamation, freeing Polly and the other slaves in the house on Franklin Street and the Montague's two plantations, but Sallie makes no mention of this. Instead, she writes of "the dawn of a bright young girlhood" in the ruins of the burned city.

In 1868, before becoming a debutante, she spent her last summer with a Montague aunt and uncle in the Adirondack Mountains, enjoying "a carefree open-air life." Returning to Richmond, she was

> in bouncing health, but looking frightfully awkward. I had outgrown all my dresses, and was burned brown as a berry. . . . Mammy often threatened to sew a sunbonnet on me if I didn't mind what she said, and stop running around bare-headed. I dreaded this, feeling that it would mean suffocation!

Sallie hastens on, describing her new frocks, dreamy pinks and blues, and her coming-out party where "young people danced merrily to the entrancing music of Kesnick's band."

A lavish feast followed the dance: "First there was a mammoth block of ice in the centre of which was carved a huge bowl filled with the best Linhaven bay oysters." The desserts were "evolved by Pizzini who reigned over party suppers," nougat baskets, and pyramids of orange slices under veils of spun sugar. Sallie concludes, "Absurd to dwell upon the luxury of the table when there was beauty of a far higher kind." That is, for Sallie "the reigning beauties of my girlhood in Richmond"—Mary Triplett, with her golden hair, classic features, and "incomparable manner"; "lovely Lizzie Cabell," with eyes "so deeply, darkly blue"; Mattie Ould "who lured men with her ready wit, and fathomless dark eyes." Other girls are described with sugared adjectives until the repetition becomes as cloying as Pizzini's desserts.

After her debut, she delighted in "a joyous summer at the old White Sulphur Springs" hotel, considering it "the very cream and perfection of a young girl's belle-ship. Riding and dancing were my chief delights, including the ever-popular morning Germans," she writes. "The German" was the crown of Richmond social life, especially for the city's debutantes, an annual series of intricate figures, like square dances, led for fifty years by former Confederate General Jo Lane Stern. At the end of the summer, Sallie was so exhausted her parents took her "to the lovely old Sweet Springs" for a rest. Like her friends, she waited to see which "admirer" would follow her.

Sallie was facing the decision that would shape the rest of her life: which of the gallants should she chose for a husband? The path to such a decision was not smooth; one suitor, "a poor inoffensive man I had been running away from for months" pursued her to her retreat, where she tried to throw him off by flirting with "a nice comfortable cousin of the family. He cared for none of us. Girls were no more to him than buttercups in a field."

Her ruse succeeded in driving off the sorry contender but then backfired: when Sallie told the cousin that he had served his purpose and could "now go back to your poor neglected classics, 'No,' said he, and as I looked up I was startled by the stern determined look on a face usually bland and contemplative. 'YOU have been playing, but not I.'"

Horrified, Sallie listened to "words too deep and true for the trifling play I demanded. I was ashamed, and when at length I reached my room flung myself down in a flood of tears. The next morning at dawn Cousin Paul rode away."

Cousin Rosalie tried to console her. "Try not to be distressed, it is not your fault, I saw it coming long ago." But if Rosalie saw it coming, why was Sallie oblivious?

Next came "winter gaieties" in Richmond, again featuring the German dances, still continuing to increase in popularity. Among the attendees were "all the sought after young men of the day," Sallie writes. Principal among the organizers was her father, John Henry Montague, who had held the first German in his double parlor on Franklin Street in 1867.

Sallie writes,

> We were quite primitive in the early stages. Dances were given
> in different private houses, carriages were not even thought of
> unless it rained, we just put our little slippers in a silk bag and
> trotted off with our escorts.

The ritual surrounding the Richmond German represented much of what was deemed important throughout Sallie's long life. The ballroom, the dancers' presentation, the role of the dance's leaders— these all invoked carefully supervised romance, intense respectability, and a consciousness of belonging to one of the First Families of Virginia, a social standing so pervasive that the group was familiarly known as FFV, no matter how straitened that family's circumstances. And yet amidst all these firmly proscribed rituals Sallie retained some of the spirit of the young girl who was once excessively tanned and who rode bareback on her family's plantations.

•

Sallie was having far too good a time to use all this gaiety for its designated end: the business of getting married.

An 1870 letter from her father reproves "my dear daughter" for discussing matrimony "with too much levity. It is one of those sublime and awful subjects about which it is not well to talk flippantly—as, one of these days, perhaps when you are grown, you may find out." At twenty, Sallie was evidently not considered "grown" by her family.

Later, John Henry wrote that he had heard from an acquaintance that

> you were certainly to be married this spring. Now, how is this? ... I am not to be consulted about a trifle of that sort? If this be so, then indeed I am as your grandma would say "A mere figure of naught."

But Sallie did not marry for seven more years, a typical delay at that time in the South, which had lost a generation of young men. She writes that, eventually, "I somehow became conscious of a slight spirit of anxiety for my future on the part of certain relatives. . . . They began to say I must be heatless." (Her granddaughter Mary's neat penciling corrects the word to "heartless" although "heatless" may have been closer to Sallie's intent.)

For Sallie, the realization dawned:

> Greatly to my amusement, the dark shade of an old maid in the family loomed before them! . . . When my father sensed this he promptly took occasion to urge me never to consider marriage until someone arrived who should be absolutely essential to my happiness.

Although Sallie was still enjoying her "bellehood . . . the idyllic state could not go on forever. My fate was approaching!"

The light touch of her exclamation points belies the importance of her subsequent meeting with a young man from Northern Ireland who had recently come to Richmond to apprentice at Colonel Robert Stiles' law firm.

Jeffrey Arthur Lefroy, or Arthur as he was called, first attracted Sallie's attention by a display of horsemanship, driving his team in tandem down a Richmond street.

"I had never seen horses driven in tandem before," Sallie writes, "and loving horses as I did, was well pleased at their beauty and spirited movement." She asked her escort if he knew the "tall blond" driver.

This young man, she learned, was an Anglo-Irish gentleman "who had come to Virginia, and would probably buy property if all things were satisfactory. I was to learn that conditions were entirely satisfactory!"

He would ultimately count a Bishop of Calcutta and Metropolitan of India—the head of the Anglican Church in that British-controlled country—as his brother, and already boasted a former lady-in-waiting to Queen Victoria as his grandmother; his family was well established in Ulster and County Meath, descendants of a family that fled from the Netherlands during the Spanish Wars, arriving in England in 1569.

Arthur's great-grandfather had been an officer in the British Army, stationed in Ireland for many years; he founded the Irish branch of the Lefroys, most of whom became rectors in the Established Irish Church, at that time a branch of the English Anglican. John Montague must have seen the advantages both to his family and to his beloved daughter in the match; he could not have known that, later, this Lefroy money would save both Sallie and her daughter from financial catastrophe, for a time.

Sallie gives no particulars of the financial arrangements accompanying her acceptance of the Irishman. Arthur, she writes, was "unselfish,

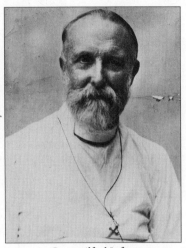

Jeffrey (Jeffry) Arthur Lefroy, married
Sallie Watson Montague, 1877

George Alfred Lefroy,
brother of Jeffrey Arthur Lefroy

manly," a man "who made the happiness of my young life, and the most sacred memories of later life."

Not quite satisfied with this brief summary from her memoir, I sifted through the blue box to see if I could find letters from Sallie's courtship. There were two that displayed, if not her and Arthur's bond, then its generous embrace in "the unfailing affection and consideration" of Arthur's "most dear and interesting family" in Ireland.

Arthur's mother, Helena Trench Lefroy, wrote to "My dear Miss Montague" on November 27, 1876, from Aghaderg, her husband's parish in County Down:

> I hear from my son Arthur that the day has been fixed for your marriage. Under these circumstances I can no longer forbear to send you a few lines to express the warm interest with which I, in common with his Father & every member of our family have heard of your engagement to our son.

Our anxious thoughts have followed him when he went from us to live among strangers in a distant land. . . .

I wish now merely to say with what pleasure we are looking forward to seeing you here (please God) next spring as his wife, and what a cordial and loving welcome you shall receive from us all.

On the same day, Arthur's sister Minna Lefroy wrote to Sallie, introducing her sister Mary:

We hope that you will try and think of us as sisters. It makes us so happy to think that Arthur has found someone to love him & make a home for him in his new country. I daresay you can easily believe he is a very dear brother to us, and that what is such a joy to him must be a joy to us too.

Neither of Arthur's sisters came to Richmond for the wedding, but his brother George attended, to Sallie's surprise. She thought the ocean voyage would deter him, to which her fiancé replied, "You don't know George." In later days, once this same George had ascended to the highest post of the Anglican Church in India, it was apparent in hindsight that a mere crossing of the Atlantic Ocean would not have daunted him.

•

I returned to the blue box again, finding an account of Sallie's honeymoon: "After our marriage we sailed for England," Sallie wrote in a letter to a friend; it was the first time she had left the United States. The ship

rolled, pitched and wallowed. I was desperately sick, but Arthur would not let me languish below. . . . He wrapped me in rugs

and carried me on deck, there securely strapped in my sea chair
I survived, being fed alternatively a spoonful of clear soup and
later iced champagne. As soon as I could speak I assured my
husband that I would come again next summer if he asked me
politely!

Presumably he did; the summer crossings became almost annual events.

After the boat docked, Sallie and Arthur set off to visit his parents
in the small Northern Ireland town of Dromore.

Sallie's father-in-law, Jeffry Lefroy—Rector of Aghaderg and Dean
of Dromore—was remembered as "the humblest of men"; he served his
church for fifty years. In 1844 he had married Helena Trench, eldest
daughter of Reverend Frederick Stewart and Lady Helena Trench,
fresh from her position as one of Queen Victoria's ladies-in-waiting,
who bore him nine children.

Helena Trench Lefroy was well educated for the period, according
to her son George's account which I also found preserved in the blue
box, and was "thoroughly grounded in the classics by her father"; she
was a botanist and learned to speak French, German, and Italian, and
was remembered as having a "noble influence" on her many children.
Deeply pious, she was so moved by one of George Augustus Selwyn's
sermons that she dedicated her "yet unborn babe" to God. This would
be George, who indeed went on to an illustrious career in the upper
echelons of the Anglican Church.

"In some ways perhaps I was unusually confiding," Sallie writes of
this first visit to Arthur's parents.

> Many brides have told me of their trepidation upon first meeting
> their husband's family, but I was saved a great deal of this, partly
> [because of] their wonderful letters, and also I think Arthur

had a singularly clear way of presenting to my imagination their lovable personalities. In all events I arrived amongst them with a perfectly child-like anticipation of affection. I quite believed that they would love me, Arthur said so, and I did not know what else they could do with me!

I will only say there was never a moment of doubt or disappointment. Father and Mother [her names for Arthur's parents] met our train and I had my first warm welcome and my first drive through the lovely Irish countryside.

"'Bow to the people, Dear,' Mother said softly" as they drove through a crowd of villagers. "Some of the men had ropes with which they intended to draw the carriage up the avenue," but the coachman objected and so Sallie missed, to her regret, this traditional rite of welcome.

"There began on that sweet spring day months of a very happy new life," made even more pleasant by its resemblance to antebellum life in Virginia. In Ireland, as at home, she was a member of a cultivated landed gentry that was happily supported, economically and physically, by an idealized peasantry.

Sallie enjoyed Dromore's "beautiful old homes, cherished old customs, and the atmosphere so redolent of all that is fascinating in old world history and romance." Uprisings that from time to time disrupted this vision of Ireland lay beyond her ken.

During her stay, Sallie paid customary visits to the women who lived in the village, going with Helena or Arthur's sisters to distribute charity, as her mother had done, from her Dorcas basket, in Richmond.

Sallie felt that, on these visits, they were greeted with the same gratitude she had learned, from all her interactions with those of lesser social standing, to expect: "I only wish I could recall the many amusing and kindly speeches of the dear good women!"

If there were undercurrents of resentment, Sallie was unaware of them, rejoicing in the "kindly offerings" of the women— "handkerchiefs, tablecloths and other such treasures" woven on household looms, which formed the foundation of Ulster's economy.

During her visit, Sallie established a special bond with her father-in-law. Years later, after Arthur's death, Dean Lefroy left four thousand pounds in a trust, the income to be given to Sallie for her use unless she married again—a common provision at the time— with half this money to pass to her daughter. The interest, at four percent, was paid to Sallie until her first grandchild reached the age of five, after which the investments were sold and the proceeds divided between Sallie and her daughter Helena, all according to the trust agreement.

These investments—in the Bengal-Nagpur Railway, the Eastern Telegraph Company, and Antigua Government Stock—were sold in 1903, and the net gain on the original four thousand pounds, minus trustee's fees, was a mere twelve pounds, eleven shillings.

Since this was an unusually small gain on the original investment, presumably Sallie drew on the principal over the years to provide for Helena and her children. My mother, Sallie's granddaughter Mary, indicated in her oral history that Sallie was living in relative poverty at the end of her life. But during Sallie's first visit with her new husband's family, she could not have known that such trials of finance and changes of fortune were in store.

•

After a few days at Dromore, Sallie and her in-laws embarked on the Lefroys' regular summer expedition to Newcastle.

As brother Charles remembered it,

the cow and the pony, and the cart with the luggage, started in the evening, [and] the family in an old-fashioned carriage began their migration next morning. Once settled in, the whole family engaged in constant excursions into the hills; they bathed and boated, of course, and it was the mother who rejoiced to arrange all the plans and picnics.

Helena read aloud to the assembled throng every evening, especially prizing the works of Sir Walter Scott and *The Heir of Redclyffe* by "Miss Yonge."

The family was accompanied by the longtime Lefroy governess, Sarah Anne Curtis, known to the children as Curtie. She spent forty-seven years with the Lefroys, raising their nine children; she told them stories from Scripture as well as Irish fairy tales, excelled in games, puzzles, and charades, and was at the same time, Sallie remembered, "a stern disciplinarian."

"The only trouble they ever had with her," Sallie claimed, "was that when the children grew up and went out into the world she missed them tearfully." But

> her spacious nursery with its bright open fire continued all through her life to be a favorite retreat for her children, even when grown to manhood and womanhood. I too fell into the habit of making an almost daily visit.

Curtie regaled her newest visitor with tales of Arthur and his siblings. Later, Curtie would extend her love to Sallie's daughter Helena "and declare she was thereby comforted for the empty years between the two generations." Curtie was a close and constant presence in Sallie's new family's life, and they seemed aware of how much they relied upon her. Sallie, in her memoir, described how her mother-in-law "used to say in her sweet way, 'I think I must have some good in me because I am not jealous of Curtie.'"

Curtie's portrait is not complete without two examples of her needlework: two square, hard pincushions. These relics from the blue box are strange in every way to a modern eye; pincushions of this kind fell out of favor with the disappearance of women's hats—and hatpins. During Curtie's lifetime, pincushions would have been a staple of every lady's dressing table, bristling with a forest of long, bejeweled, and jet-tipped hatpins.

Curtie made her two pincushions out of the same scrap of green silk. Once a bright green, the silk has faded over the course of its 150 years, and her embroidery, fashioned out of tiny green beads, has lost its sparkle. The older of the two pincushions is edged with darker green ruching, its folds set with beads, while the later pincushion is bordered with now-dingy lace. The beaded motto on the older pincushion reads,

> Oh, may the eye ne'er closed
>> in sleep
>>> watch over babe and mother keep.

Beaded beneath these lines is "1852," the date of Arthur Lefroy's birth, which made him two years younger than Sallie. A silent self-consciousness about their age difference could be the reason why her birthday was sometimes erroneously recorded as 1852.

Sallie and Arthur's daughter Helena's birth in 1878 is commemorated by the newer pincushion, beaded with a similar sentiment:

> Good angels hover
>> over babe and mother.

Curtie, who has vanished so completely in other ways—leaving no portrait, no letters, no diary, her employers' memories long extinguished by their deaths—still exerts her presence in these pincushions, and in the written memories of her charges' letters and Sallie's memoir, in the blue box.

After the Ireland visit, Arthur and Sallie went to Paris. They stayed with Arthur's aunt Mary Lefroy, sightseeing every day and invited to "nice little dinner parties" almost every evening. Sallie wrote in a letter home:

> I have met some charming people, principally English, whom I find as cordial and pleasant as possible; in fact it seems to me a person's modesty and unaffectedness of manner only increases in proportion to his rank. The shyest man I've met at all was an English Earl of great wealth whose face flushed with gratification whenever a lady spoke to him, even on the most conventional subjects.

At the opera:

> The whole audience was in full dress, so I had ample opportunity of examining French toilets, the principal feature of which is its extreme simplicity, at least in comparison with Americans.

And in the shops:

> My shopping is still in a crude state, but you will be glad to know my money seems holding out excellently. . . . Aunt Mary is a very

shrewd business woman and knows the French shopkeepers too well to give them a penny more than is necessary.

In May, she wrote her brother Johnnie in "Amerique" from the Hotel Belle Vue on the Lac de Como. She was being "rewarded" for what "I was rather disposed to regard as my heroism in leaving Paris" by "the very beautiful and fashionable summer resort" where she and Arthur were staying. Then they had to change hotels because Arthur complained that at the Hotel Belle Vue

> their plates were cold, their boats clumsy, and I think above all there was a woman in supreme command of affairs, which later, with the usual complimentary opinion of your sex, for our business capacity, he announced in an ex cathedra manner would inevitably give us trouble in the settling of our bill, however small.

Back in London, Arthur took her to his old school and introduced her to

> such a number of old friends, boys and masters, that I found myself in the astonishing position of belle! Everybody wanted to see "Arty's wife"—they declared that I did not know the masters from the boys, and seemed quite amused at my talking the same nonsense to one as to the other.

Arthur, unlike Sallie, left no memoir. There was only one letter in his hand in the blue box, written to his mother Helena from the Galt House in Cincinnati, Ohio, four years after his marriage. He had just received her letter with "the sad news of my dear grandmother's death."

Lady Helena Trench had lived to be eighty-eight; at eighty, she had still walked a mile to church and back every Sunday. Asked how she felt on her deathbed, she had replied, "Oh! Failing, failing, failing; but oh! How I wish that matters would hurry up a little."

Arthur wrote,

> I was much startled and overcome by the news. . . . Her peaceful end was symbolical of her life, and I was grateful that there had been no acute suffering at the last. We have all of us lost the truest friend that a lot of boys ever had.

He had been in Lexington, Kentucky,

> buying some valuable horses for some rich people in New York and Boston, who give us carte blanche so long as we get them the perfect article. We are on our way to New York now, with 14 head of perfect beauties.

This energetic letter carries no hint of the disease that would kill Arthur three years later. He may have been temporarily free of the symptoms—coughing, fatigue, weight loss—of the dread disease that was known as The White Plague, or he may simply have learned to ignore them.

The German bacteriologist Robert Koch identified the tubercle bacillus in 1882, five years after Arthur and Sallie's marriage. In its early stages, tuberculosis can display few symptoms; Arthur must still have seemed healthy when he went to Virginia.

There was no hint of worry about Arthur's health in Sallie's description of her extended honeymoon in 1877. Her one concession to his eventual disease occurs in a brief anecdote in her memoir. She confesses that, as a newlywed, she did indulge in "certain careless habits which disquieted my husband's orderly mind. The worse of me was that I frequently wrote letters on my lap!"

Arthur told her, "sitting all doubled up was unhealthy, bad for my lungs."

> "Lungs?" I said. "Oh, I never thought about lungs."
> "Well," said he, "they are rather worth thinking about."

Although Sallie had promised Arthur to return to Ireland every year, the young couple stayed in Richmond during the summer of 1878 because of the impending birth of their daughter, Helena Trench Lefroy—my grandmother.

Helena provided, Sallie writes, "the joy of my youth, the pride of our household, and the solace of my old age."

Helena's birth did not hinder Sallie from resuming her daily rides on her favorite horse, "my beloved Jennie Dean"; she still found it "delightful flying, as it seemed, over fences and ditches."

"When Helena was two years old we sailed again for Ireland," Sallie writes, "Arthur wanted his daughter to have her Irish relatives impressed upon her mind and heart" while she was still very young. But there was another reason for urgency.

"Again we had a stormy voyage," Sallie continues, but two-year-old Helena was "fearless." The steamship at times went under sail, and when the sailors were hauling up canvas, they left "a short end of rope for the baby to pull and join in their work," chanting along with the men, "Hey, ho, blow the man down." Helena even had a little sailor suit.

"I have always been glad of this second visit to our dear ones," Sallie writes in her memoir. It would be Arthur's last.

His illness had become impossible to ignore: "The blow was struck and my life seemed to fall in pieces before me." Sallie immediately adds, "But I will not dwell on this to you, my dear young hearts"—her grand-daughters—and so she omits even the name of Arthur's disease.

The young couple was told by a London doctor to go to the South of France, warm weather being the only antidote then known to a rapid decline from what was certainly tuberculosis. In the Hôtel Beau Rivage in Cannes, they joined a host of invalids and their attendants.

In her memoir, Sallie refuses to focus on her "sadness and apprehension," describing instead their stay at a "desirable little family hotel" in Cannes. "We had a wonderful outdoor life" in the mild winter weather, sitting in the hotel garden or walking and driving with new friends; Sallie particularly appreciated "the quickness and complaisance of the French."

It had been wrenching to leave two-year-old Helena in Ireland with her grandparents and Curtie. In the blue box, I found a tiny note, addressed to "Miss Helena Trench Lefroy, care of Curtie, The Nursery," which hints at the sadness of this first separation.

"My darling little Baby Daughter," Sallie wrote in her gentle cursive,

> Papa and Mama were so happy when the Post-Master brought your nice letter. What a grand Helena to be sure, to write letters. Please write another to tell Mama that yr cold is quite well. You must remember all about your beautiful Xmas tree, and yr two parties.

One party, Helena would describe in a later letter, "for little poor children," another "for little better children."

Sallie promised that they will return to Ireland "when Papa is well and strong."

Later that winter, Curtie wrote to Sallie that Helena "can now talk of you without fretting, and has a party every night with your pictures, saying, 'That's my great big papa, he's such a handsome fellow!'"

Sallie wrote her mother reassuringly,

> Arthur is so much more comfortable here, he breathes the light
> soft air more naturally, and with much less effort, he says it is
> delightful not to have to think of each breath as he did in Ireland.
> A careful, regular life with no excitement will do all that can be
> done to cure his heart trouble.

"Heart trouble" was a subterfuge to prevent her family from knowing the terrible truth. Since at this time a tendency to tuberculosis was thought to be inherited, she would not have wanted to introduce that alarm to her family—or possibly to herself.

Arthur was still smoking and, as Sallie wrote, "torturing himself by picturing the delicious pure weed which Papa and the boys [her younger brothers] were smoking down in the dining room about now." Although now unable to climb stairs, Arthur never gave up his pipe.

Even as she worried about her husband's illness, Sallie found ways to entertain herself and Arthur as he took his cure, and also to turn what could have been days of heartbreak into sweet, funny stories. In her memoir, Sallie tells a story about another resident of their hotel, a wheelchair-bound man visited by a lady with "a quiet modest manner. I liked her."

When Sallie remarked that the two are in love, Arthur remonstrated, "My dear child, what are you thinking of? He should never marry, it would not be honorable in that condition."

"Now, Arthur, listen to me, you are not usually so conventional," Sallie retorted. "Try not to take a material view. I think she is a 'perfect woman, nobly planned'"—perhaps wisely omitting the next line of Wordsworth's poem, which ends "to command"—"and only longs to sacrifice everything to share his life and companionship," as she was doing for Arthur.

Then she announced, "I shall see what it feels like proposing to a man!"

"More power to you," Arthur said.

"Watch me proposing," Sallie replied, "but from a safe distance."

Faced with the loss of her husband, Sallie acted with the verve that was already her hallmark, and arranged a marriage for a stranger with another invalid.

She finishes her tale: "To end a long story, in a few weeks it was all happily settled," resulting in the inevitable "radiant bride and happy groom."

Arthur lived for four more years after their sojourn in Cannes, but after these stories he disappears from Sallie's reminiscences. The young woman who never saw mutilated soldiers in her father's Civil War hospital edits out the last stages of her husband's illness. Perhaps she was able to protect her daughter Helena, as well, from the harrowing details of her father's death, which occurred in Richmond in the winter of 1884, when Helena was six.

Arthur was buried in the Montague family plot in Hollywood Cemetery. His grave provided a site for family visits, as it could not have done in Ireland, keeping some vestige of his memory alive for his daughter. Sallie remarked later that Helena seemed to remember her father clearly, although she was so young when he died.

During the first summer of her widowhood, Sallie could not face going back to Ireland. Instead, she took Helena and a nurse to one of the West Virginia resorts, with plenty of books to keep the little girl occupied. Still, when the Friday evening train brought the fathers up from Richmond, Helena would mourn, "Everybody has a father but me." Later in her life, Helena would also remember the women washing their long hair on Thursday nights and leaning over the hotel's balconies to dry it, preparing for Friday reunions.

Sallie and Helena sailed for Ireland the next summer, in 1886, establishing a lifelong habit. Sallie wrote to her mother on black-bordered mourning paper, but transcended its gloom in describing "our wedding"—Arthur's brother Harry's in Dublin.

She very nearly stole the show:

> Everyone made such a fuss over me because I came all the way
> from Virginia for the wedding. I wore my new white serge which
> had not appeared before and a soft little white silk bonnet I made
> for the occasion and got kisses and compliments enough from all
> the brothers to puff me up for a month! Dare say I'll go down a
> little by the time I get home so don't be uneasy!

•

Her widow's weeds gave Sallie special status and even a certain allure;
because Queen Victoria had adopted black after Prince Albert's death
in 1861, wearing it until her death in 1901, public mourning had
become fashionable—and expensive. A widow needed to replace all
her clothes with black garments in the newest style. However, after two
years a widow was allowed to go into demi-mourning, as Sallie had,
wearing gray, lavender, or white.

Sallie wrote, "Helena is happy and running wild. She thinks all her
uncles are built for her exclusive amusement and use and Uncle George's
shoulders are expected to do pretty constant duty in place of a pony."

In a postscript, Sallie added,

> Helena is such an April day child! I read her Papa's messages
> which pleased and amused her so much, then all in a moment
> she put down her head, and burst into a flood of tears, explaining
> afterwards that she could not bear to think of GdPapa being all
> alone, and she thought she should be there because there was no
> woman in the house to take care of him!

Sallie and little Helena went back to Richmond at the end of the summer, taking up residence in the Montague house on Franklin Street where they would live for many years.

In 1894, ten years after Arthur's death, Sallie ventured into unknown territory, joining the newly formed Richmond Woman's Club, an act the Club—which exists to this day with a current membership of 1,500—describes as "courageous." Because notions of propriety were, at the time, so restrictive, few women with social standing ventured outside their homes alone, much less declared that they were meeting in private to better themselves as individuals.

The Richmond Woman's Club's fourteen founding members came from the city's elite; many lived as Sallie did on East Franklin Street.

Elected to the board in 1895, Sallie was one of the Club's first members and served for a time as its president. She surely endorsed the club's aims: to enjoy "the delightful friction of well-trained minds"—as the club's first president, Jane Looney (later Lewis), expressed it—at weekly sessions devoted to "Music, Dramatic Performance and Literature."

Invitations from those early years promised two entertainments a month; the club house, first established in a rented space on West Main Street, also offered its members a place to gather socially, the club having made tea, magazines, and newspapers available for its members.

Speakers on many subjects were invited to the weekly late afternoon meetings, refreshments were served (for which, at least initially, Sallie was responsible, as a note to herself attests: "Get someone to serve tea and coffee") and thus an atmosphere of "collegiality" was nurtured.

By 1900, the Richmond Woman's Club's membership had

grown to such a degree and its financial resources were so much strengthened that it was able to buy the handsome Bolling Haxall House at 211 Franklin Street. By 1915, sufficient resources enabled the membership to approve and see completed the addition of a large ballroom, increasing the club's seating capacity by several hundred.

The Club included two groups of women: one composed of those like Sallie who were primarily interested in socializing and self-improvement, and another, committed to influencing the society around them. The first group objected to joining the General Federation of Women's Groups, finding that organization too political because of its support for suffrage.

Over time, and despite members' early reluctance, the Club took on various progressive causes, from funding a scholarship for a "poor Virginia mountain girl" to working for the Richmond Public Library, the Visiting Nurses Association, prison reform, and better conditions for working women.

There was always opposition, however, from the group that was more comfortable with literary and musical events; Sallie was probably one of those who rapped their umbrellas on the floor to silence a speaker they felt was too political.

The Club's reputation in Richmond was impeccable, although Sallie notes in her memoir that in the beginning there were

> a few who professed to be shocked at the very thought of a woman's club! Could our "ladies" indulge in anything so essentially masculine? Some horrified elderly gentlemen pictured nightly orgies over the selling of liquid refreshment!

In case her granddaughters were equally concerned, Sallie hastens to explain, "The sole indulgence was in literary and historical lectures, and the liquid refreshment was imported from China!"

Sallie was a member of the Richmond Woman's Club for twenty-seven years. In an official club portrait taken in 1907, halfway through her term as an active member, Sallie looks extraordinarily assured, her sculpted lips set. At fifty-seven, her creamy skin is shown to advantage in the scoop neck of her black silk gown. Her dark blond hair is arranged becomingly in a chignon, with curls tendriling across her forehead; her beautifully set eyes express calm confidence.

Sallie W. Montague's official portrait, 1907
Richmond Women's Club

Throughout her tenure, both as member and as president, Sallie focused her formidable energies on the Club, especially on the choice of speakers; she often introduced them. I was astonished to find all seventy-two of her carefully penned introductions preserved in the blue box.

The number of women invited to the podium was unusual for that period. This followed member Mary Munford's 1896 suggestion to the board that more women speakers be featured. As the podium was increasingly taken by female authors, artists, and scholars, a growth in self-confidence by the membership at large seemed assured—at least when the speakers read their scholarly papers themselves; one woman refused, insisting on recruiting a substitute presenter.

Sallie's undated introductions, far more than her memoir, convey her curiosity, energy, and intellectual vigor.

Each of the seventy-two was written in rapid, flowing cursive on small sheets of paper; she used one side only, and folded each page into fourths, the folds so crisp that they retain their compact shape after more than a hundred years. They are small enough to fit in a lady's reticule.

One typical introduction asks the audience to welcome John Skelton Williams "who has kindly consented to talk to us of the 'Illumination of Manuscripts.'" Sallie describes the speaker as "one whose discriminating taste and artistic abilities have had the advantage of old-world culture." She continues:

> I make it a rule never to entrench upon the subject of a
> Lecturer, bearing in mind who they are that "rush in." But for
> this salutary self-discipline, I would now grow enthusiastic
> upon the beauties of a most ancient art. This, however, I leave
> to one much better qualified to illustrate its merits.

Later, when she began to write her own essays, she claimed, with reason, to be as qualified as any speaker she had previously introduced. Sometimes there were last-minute cancellations; Sallie refers to "the best laid plans of mice and men" in explaining to her audience

> that today has not brought us the expected distinguished
> stranger, but happily we of the Woman's Club have no need
> to play Mariana in the moated grange and wail, "He cometh
> not."

She could count on her audience to recognize her quote from Tennyson's poem "Mariana," as she prepares her audience for their replacement speaker, announcing, "We turn with serene confidence to talent within our own borders" in the person of Mrs. William G.

Stanard "who at the last moment has kindly responded to our urgent appeal & will read a paper upon...." The last-minute change left no time to provide Sallie with the title.

The Club and its members weathered other uneasy moments together.

On the publication of the eighth edition of the local *Hardy Annual* (edited by John Montague, Sallie's father, and which poked fun at the Club's members), Sallie warns, "We may well tremble in terror.... Had I been dipped like Achilles in the River Styx, still would their winged shafts of wit find and pierce my most vulnerable heel." Again, she knew her audience would recognize her reference to the classic Greek story.

Such mild self-deprecation was a sure bond. Sallie begins one introduction with a story about herself:

> Only the memory of a little incident encourages me today. On being presented to a distinguished author whose book I loved, I tried to tell her so, but was met with such a tired look.... I made a desperate plunge, changed the subject & commended the beauty of her gown! Instantly, a real human hand grasped my trembling hand, and a rush of warm pleasure lighted the erstwhile cold face. She too was a woman! So encouraged was I that I ran home and wrote a story myself!

The ensuing story has not survived, but seven essays, delivered to the club when her turn came as speaker, are preserved in the blue box. Her subjects were drawn from a wide range of topics, and included relatively obscure historical figures as well as widely perceived problems with changing modern mores.

Speaking on a sixteenth-century French poet, Clément Marot, Sallie sets the stage for her listeners:

> It was the palmy time of Rhétoriqueurs, poets who combined
> stilted & pedantic language with an obstinate adherence to
> the allegorical manner of the fifteenth century, & to the most
> complicated and artificial forms of the Ballade & Rondeau.

Her talk on manners again depends on an audience well-versed
in the classics, as it is studded with quotations from Chesterfield,
Emerson, Shakespeare, and Goethe.

Citing manners as "the principles governing the intercourse of the
best people," Sallie implies that manners were solely in the province
of society's upper echelons, even as distinctions between classes were
beginning to evaporate around her; she would not have believed that
her own future descendants would hardly dare claim to be, or even to
know, "the best people."

Manners, she writes, have "crystallized into words that carry a
connotation of absolute authority and perfection." She cites Goethe's
"a politeness of the heart," which might also be called love. More than
her conviction regarding manners' exclusivity, she would pass on
her overarching faith in the power of good manners to shape unruly
emotions for kinder and worthier ends.

Sallie's seven essays, each a lecture she presented, are tied up with a
half hitch, a reminder of the knots she learned as a horsewoman. When
I untied the delicate cord, I realized the knot had held for more than a
hundred years, the essays left unread by any of her descendants.

Yet these folded papers mark, for me, the beginning of the era
that might free my grandmother and my mother from many of the
constraints—an inability to admit pain, for instance, and a constant
conflation of worth and race and economic class—that limit Sallie's
memoir, which she chose to end, strangely and abruptly, with the story
of a hanging her father witnessed when he was a child.

"There were pirates in those long ago days," Sallie writes, placing the story before 1824 when a concerted effort by the United States and the British Navy ended the operation of pirates along Virginia's Atlantic Coast. Her father, then, was not older than ten when this story took place. "There was great excitement when three Portuguese 'pirates' were at last captured, imprisoned in Richmond, tried and condemned to death."

Her father, called here "little Johnnie boy," and his nurse were brought by the nurse's boyfriend to witness the pirates' hanging on a hill near Hollywood Cemetery, which, Sallie notes, "might have had a bad effect had he been a delicate or timid child."

Her father had "all too clear a view of the gruesome sight of the three miserable figures as they dangled against the sky. Johnnie was very silent on the way back." That night he woke screaming. Comforted by his mother's maid and his mother, the little boy "in his baby talk was saying he did not want 'pirates.'"

Next day, his mother's maid beat the nurse who'd taken the child to the hanging with "an ominous switch."

Why did Sallie enclose "pirates" in quotation marks, and thus raise a question about whom the boy really saw? Looking back through history's haze, I cannot know for sure.

Lynching statistics only began to be gathered in 1882; between that date and 1968, at least 3,446 African Americans were hanged, burned, and shot, untried, for largely imaginary crimes. During this period and well before, going to a lynching was, for white Southerners such as Sallie's family, a social event, and white children were often in the crowd. Whether "little Johnnie boy" saw a slave or a pirate dangling against the sky, this story finally breaks the smooth surface of Sallie's memoir.

Having nearly completed her memoir for her granddaughters, Sallie must have recognized on some level how much she had left out. Though she may not have intended it to, her description of the hanging signifies the gap, as when ancient cartographers wrote in the yet-to-be-explored spaces on their maps, "Here be monsters."

Pirates will turn up again in one of her daughter Helena's short stories, whose pirate hero rescues a lady dying from cholera. He's first seen lying naked on the deck of his ship, the wind blowing on his ivory-white body. Satanic, lifesaving, he hardly seems a near relative of the three men whose hanging terrified the writer's grandfather. And yet there is a link: dark enchantment, punishment, pain, and suffering—

Four generations of Montagues, circa 1900
Melinda (l.), Sallie (standing), Helena (seated) with
her first child, Arthur Lefroy Caperton

all of which Sallie carefully avoids—will become the stuff of her daughter Helena's fiction.

Here Sallie's reminiscences end. She lived until 1942, posing around 1900 for a portrait of four generations: Melinda Fox Montague, Sallie Montague Lefroy, Helena Montague Caperton, and a small boy, Arthur Lefroy Caperton, Sallie's only grandson.

Long after Sallie's death—which came fifty-eight years after her husband Arthur's—Helena told me a story that pointed to her mother's enduring capacity to have fun. When Buffalo Bill brought his Wild West Show to Richmond in the late 1880's, Sallie caught the showman's eye as he drove his Dead Wood Coach around the arena. Somehow, Bill managed an introduction, and Sallie was invited to ride with him the next day. Then he left town. Later, he sent her a riding crop whose silver top was engraved with her initials.

Helena gave me the crop. I like to imagine Sallie on horseback, recapturing, in her moment beside Buffalo Bill, the free and easy feeling of flying that she'd so often enjoyed as a child.

TWO

Slotted into the hilly Hollywood graveyard in Richmond, Virginia, lie the remains of my grandmother, Sallie's daughter, Helena Lefroy Caperton, in a concrete box.

She shares a tall, grim monument with her husband, my long-forgotten grandfather, Clifford Randolph Caperton, who died in a car accident on May 5, 1939, leaving his widow with seven grown children and very little money outside of a ten-thousand-dollar life insurance policy.

Born on August 18, 1878, in her Montague grandparents' house at 118 East Franklin Street in Richmond, Helena grew up as the widowed Sallie's only child, among Montague relatives who seemed never to leave home.

Helena's education does not merit much detail in her mother's memoir; unlike Sallie, Helena was never expected to work, even briefly. "In studies she liked, naturally she had good marks," Sallie writes in her memoir, but "an unfortunate aversion to math never lessened."

Helena Trench Lefroy as a young child

Happily, "the day came when [Helena's] studies in literature were a delight almost as much to me as to her." Reading aloud provided the essential emotional link between Helena and her mother, as well as with Helena's maternal grandfather, John Henry Montague; he was so attached to his granddaughter, and so indulgent of her, that he insisted on her sharing the grownups' meals long before Sallie felt Helena's manners were equal to these occasions. The little girl experienced the power of words for the first time around that mahogany dinner table.

Helena Trench Lefroy in sailor cap

"Beautiful language," as in the language of the King James Bible, of Shakespeare, and the high rhetorical style of the classics, was of great value in these family exchanges, and topics and points of view that could not be expressed in beautiful language were not addressed.

The archaic quality of this family parlance was reinforced by the belief that "contemporary" talk—slang, elisions, nonstandard usage—weakened language's inherent power: to shape, control, and command.

This belief held sway throughout Richmond's white upper-class "First Families of Virginia," of which the Montagues were honored members.

The letters that bound one relative to another, and that were preserved in the blue box, were shaped by this tradition. This reverence for tradition and the strictures of formality would shape, and shackle, Helena, as she became the family's first professional writer.

As she grew up, Helena may have felt cramped in the Montague house, occupied as it was by her grandparents, her mother, several uncles and an aunt, and a formidable African-American woman named Mary Jefferson. But she remembered the house as a snug haven where she spent hours with her grandfather. Several of the short stories Helena published in the 1950s are memory pieces set in the comfortable atmosphere of East Franklin Street.

Helena at fifteen years, 1893

In one such story, "The Rake," the young narrator describes being allowed to miss church because of "the extreme cold."

> I rose from the breakfast table rejoicing. All one could do was to gaze out of the parlor window upon Franklin Street grey and deserted, and curl down deliciously beside the fire, and read *The Heavenly Twins*, which had been forbidden as corrupting. This I did, and found the book correspondingly dull.

In a basement dining room, the narrator is delighted by the news that their Sunday guest, the rake himself, is not coming. She is thrilled to be able to eat "my Sunday dinner without averting my eyes from those famished eyes, from those shaking white hands." When her grandmother worries that the missing guest might have frozen to death in his unheated room, the narrator bursts out, "I hope he did!" One glance from her grandfather is enough to "cast me out of paradise," and she runs up to her bedroom and flings herself on her bed, in tears. After a while, her grandfather comes to accept her apologies and to tell her a story from his youth that redeems the rake's virtue: he married a young girl who was dying of consumption, out of pity.

Though the title implies otherwise, the tale of the rake's history is less powerful than the grandfather's unspoken criticism. Helena would become an opinionated, even impetuous young woman but, as in her story, "one glance" from a man she admired would usually silence her.

She was an outgoing, at times unruly little girl, and Sallie, according to her memoir, took disciplining her very seriously. But Helena had her ways of dealing with her mother's discipline, explaining,

> I think you have very nice punishments when I do wrong. You put me to bed in the daytime, and I just look and look at the treetops and the sky, and then I have such beautiful thinks. I hardly mind at all.

Her formation as a writer began during those "thinks."

Summer always brought a visit to her father's family in Ireland. In preparation for one of these trips abroad, Helena concealed a box of bugs among her mother's "snowy underwear" in a trunk bound for Ireland, prompting Sallie to observe that her daughter "apparently never shared my fear and dislike of insects." After a while, Helena confessed to her mother, exclaiming, "Well, that box! It has some very nice interesting creatures I want to take over and find a home for them on Grandmother's lawn."

Careful not to "hurt the child's feelings or quench her interest in entomology," Sallie told Helena, "These poor things will never live to reach Grandmother's lawn. . . . Then, dear, just think of the happy families you are breaking up."

Helena agreed to let the bugs loose close to where she found them after her mother told her, "They have their ways of calling one another and some of them may be happy again."

In Ireland, Helena, who wept at parting from her African-American nursemaid in Richmond, was turned over to Curtie. The old governess told her the stories that would furnish her imagination: stories of Webspinner, the "miser old" who lies in wait in his web for the ancient widow, Maggie de la Moth—"He had eaten the flesh off her bones, and drunk her heart's blood." Stories of Tom, who kills an ogre with exploding cakes. "The Toad's Journal"—"Awakened, felt chilly, crept under a stone / Was vastly contented with living alone." And "The Princess Discontent," who has to wash, dress up, and act obliging before she gets the prince.

At Dromore, Helena played with her cousins. Sallie wanted her daughter to be "treated as one of themselves . . . even to the point of pulling curls and knocking her about. The better for Helena in the long run."

Helena's unpublished "Memories of an Ulster Childhood," preserved in the blue box, describes her experiences more elaborately.

She writes that on a charitable visit to the local poorhouse with Curtie, she saw a girl about her own age dying of "the white death of Ireland, tuberculosis, that struck without warning both cottage and hall"—the same disease that struck down her father.

She tiptoed toward the girl's bed "with my ineffectual little nosegay of corn flowers, and Sweet William." A matron intervened, warning, "The likes of you mustn't touch the likes of her, little lady."

At that, "Swift, overpowering indignation and pity seized me, and I shook off the old crone's hand. . . . I saw that the girl's eyes were open, and fixed upon my face."

Helena took the girl's hand, and a moment later,

she raised her head from the pillow, and held out her arms in welcome and ecstasy to some sure and certain vision. . . . Then the light was extinguished in a profound peace, her head fell upon the pillow. . . .

This unknown girl had bequeathed to me the unshakable conviction and belief in an ultimate glory. . . .

If a secure and happy childhood fortresses the mind . . . then this revelation that would so shock the "child specialist" has been my greatest source of reliance and strength.

The girl's coffin was placed at the foot of her bed, a poorhouse habit that made Helena

clench my teeth and my hands. . . . In no sense could it be camouflaged. . . . Rough-hewn, and of the classic shape, wide at the shoulders, narrow at the feet, and with four rope handles on each side . . . lined with a little straw, and the lid lay parallel, with eight heavy iron screws lying upon it ready to be driven into place.

In the introduction to one of her two collections of short stories, Helena states that Ireland, her father's country, made her a writer.

During her visits, her grandparents Dean Lefroy and his wife Helena supervised, instructed, and loved the little girl, as did her father's unmarried sister, Minna, who became a lifelong friend.

In "Memories of an Ulster Childhood," Helena describes a pony cart and pair of ponies given to her by the dean. Her essay recalls "their hard little foreheads, where each one had a black star, and their brown eyes were so soft, and lashes so long. . . ." Then she describes the first time she took them out: "It's driving of the wee beasties you will be wanting to do now?" asked John, the stableman.

He opened the door in the back of the cart, and as one in a dream I got in and he put the reins in my hands, showing me the correct form. The whip in my right hand on top of my left (although never never will I whip the darlings, I thought, although I changed my mind later). John gave a hissing whistle, and the eight little hooves twinkled off down the drive. The Lodge keeper's little girl ran out and opened the gate, and we trotted out onto the Dublin road.

The adventurous little girl must have enjoyed a landscape marked and marred by ruined castles, forts, and battle sites. The name of the area, Aghaderg, means "Red Field" and sprung from a fourth-century battle between the Three Collas and the Kingdom of Ulster that legends say left the fields stained with blood.

On one expedition, with her two boy cousins, she set out to visit family in the town of Killiney:

> It took us two days and two nights, and until noon on the third day, and every mile of it was utter happiness. There is a saying that Ireland is inhabited by men, women, and Trenches and as we were children of the clan, there were cousins' houses at which we might spend the nights.
>
> We had a favorite picnic spot [in Killiney], high in the heather, with a brown trout stream and an old round tower overlooking the bay. . . . The boys would wander upstream lazily casting their lines while my cousin Moria and I busied ourselves domestically boiling the kettle for tea, and cutting cake and sandwiches.

One day the cousins found Gypsies camping at their favorite spot. Helena describes the Gypsies with all the romanticization endemic to her time, asserting that in their camp there was nothing to suggest poverty. . . . The bright, freshly painted caravan rested, its shafts down, white muslin curtains blowing from its small windows. The horses were tethered to a nearby rowan tree. No Irish Gypsy ever has any but the best horse-flesh, exactly how they come by it is better not to inquire too closely.

A "darkly beautiful young man" wearing a chrome-yellow shirt, open at the throat, and gold earrings, greeted the children by sweeping "us a bow which was all courteous satire"; none of them understood what he said, and he remarked that "the gentry have not the speech."

When one of the boy cousins tried to reprimand him—"You know that you are trespassing, my good man?"—the Gypsy replied that the "young Lordship would not grudge us the air, the sea, the sky, the heather for a night's lodging."

"The speech was humble," Helena observed, "but his black eyes, the stance of his vibrant body, the turbulent timbre of his voice held nothing but pride."

They shared a meal, but while they were eating, the children became aware of what Helena described as

> a gentle overtone from one of the tethered horses. It would turn and look at us, and give a soft whinny, almost, it seemed of recognition.

To explain the suspicious nature of the horse's whinny, Helena explains:

> In Ireland you know your own and your neighbor's animals, as you do your human friends. In reporting a meeting with one or the other of them, you do not say, "I saw William Alyosus in the village this morning," you say, "It's the roan gelding of William Alyosus, and himself with it, that I was seeing in the village."

After their dinner an old Gypsy woman read their palms, "and we crossed hers with a silver half-crown, and what she told us became shockingly true in after years." As the children drove away, they wondered about the horse that seemed to recognize them.

Cousin Padric observed, "That was Uncle Henry's Connemara mare." The others protested that Uncle Henry's mare was a dapple gray that broke its legs and had to be shot. But, in Helena's memory, Padric knows better.

Helena was often left in the care of Curtie when her mother went to France for a part of the summer. The Irishwoman disciplined in only one way: when a child was naughty, she said, "If you are naughty you are ill, and if you are ill, you need a liquorish powder." Helena describes the liquorish powder and its administration:

> Now a liquorish powder was without a doubt the most revolting and nauseous drug a child ever had to swallow. It was administered in a dessert spoon, mixed with black currant jam. Our grownup aunts and uncles used to shudder and leave the room, unable to endure the sight of it being administered.

With Curtie, there were also weekly visits to the poorhouse, which required walking three and a half miles each way, rain or shine, an experience that the grown Helena asserts in "Memories," would "fill the modern young mother with horror." For her part, though,

> I cannot see that it did us any harm to have to face the harsh realities of life, teaching us to use pity as a motive and not an emotion. Ghoulish as it may seem, I always looked forward to it with pleasure, not morbid pleasure, but a staunch feeling

>of satisfaction that we were helping those less fortunate than ourselves . . . doing my duty in that state of life in which it had pleased God to call me

as she had learned in the Anglican catechism.

Before each of these visits, Helena picked flowers, gathered up packets of tea, sugar, and tobacco and collected "enchanting animals" carved by Simon the butler: "Simon could take a large white turnip, and carve a lamb so lifelike even to its pure wool that it might almost leap from the basket."

She adds, "There was one feature that I now agree might have been omitted, and that was our half hour with the mental cases."

Curtie would suggest that Helena wait in the garden, but "morbidly perhaps I always went with her when she read a chapter of the Bible to those poor mindless yet utterly harmless old women," mentally ill inmates who sat against the wall "mouthing and sucking loudly" the sugar candy Helena brought. The adult Helena might question the wisdom of allowing a child to visit these patients, but these parts of her poorhouse visits lingered vividly in her mind.

Not all these elderly patients were peaceable. One believed Helena had "stolen, slaughtered and eaten her beloved pig, so that she had to be forcibly restrained from doing me physical hurt, and I in consequence had my first sight of a strait-jacket."

Another old woman's "hallucination consisted in the conviction that she was a Billy Goat. I suppose it was horrid of me but I used to look forward to these performances with wicked glee." Once the matron had locked the visitors into the ward, Curtis would "move a chair to the center of the room, gathering her skirts around her and putting on her spectacles":

At the first sound of Holy Writ, there would proceed from a

corner of the room a loud "Baa baa" and galloping on all fours with a sheep skin tied around her neck would advance the old woman with the goat hallucination. . . . Curtie's timing was perfect, for as she read she had the corner of her eye on Madame Goat, and just as with a resounding baa and butt, the chair went flying across the room, Curtie would rise majestically, still reading, while chair and Billy Goat ricocheted against the opposite wall.

Weak with laughter, I would retrieve it and place it in the middle of the room, Curtie would seat herself without pause in her reading, and all the while the Billy Goat watched us, only waiting to repeat the performance.

The rest of her vacation's adventures at Aghaderg were considerably more sedate. Her uncle George Lefroy, Bishop of Calcutta, often visited—an imposing presence, although Helena, who often rode on his shoulders, enjoyed his more human side.

Years later, in an article called "Time Gambols on Withall," published in the *Richmond Review*, Helena wrote, "I heard him [the Bishop] answer a very pretty woman in a way that ran counter to what I knew he felt on the subject"—they had been speaking of heaven. "From that moment I loved him with comprehension and a sense of fellowship that never abated." For all her family's emphasis on rigor and tradition, that the respected churchman would bend his convictions to charm a pretty woman charmed Helena as well.

Then there was her ninety-nine-year-old great-uncle Anthony Lefroy at Carriglass Manor in County Down. Helena writes,

My first remembered sight of Uncle Anthony was of his being hoisted onto Centaur [his horse] by four grooms. Curtie and I were feeding the pouter pigeons in the stable yard, and we heard his roaring from afar. . . . He stumbled slowly into the yard, his valet on one side, one of his footmen on the other, neither quite daring to support him

while he cursed them for his disability.

It was too late for me and Curtie to escape and I watched fascinated as amid struggles and hoistings, and laying on of Uncle Anthony's crop upon their shoulders, the four boys got him up into his saddle. . . . [Once mounted,] he was magnificent and so was Centaur as he arched his neck and pawed the cobblestones.

Noticing the little girl, Uncle Anthony

screwed his monocle into his eye and regarded me fiercely, and I, never having been frightened by anyone, stared back at him.

"Ha," he bellowed, "hand that up to me," and pointed with his crop. One of the stablemen lifted me up. . . . Uncle Anthony smelt deliciously of bay rum and good leather.

"So you are the American niece, no by God, you are my great-grandniece, I must be getting toward middle age," Uncle Anthony said.

"I'm not American, I'm Virginian . . . and County Down," I added tactfully. "I like the way you smell." I turned my head and sniffed his coat.

His great laughter scattered the pigeons. "A gal after my own heart, suppose we elope."

And they were away, in spite of

Curtie's white frightened face . . . the wind keening in my ears. At the first fence, I felt the strong leap of Centaur . . . and the firm hold of Uncle Anthony's arms. . . . I squealed with delight.

Later, Helena's grandmother reproved him, "This is simply outrageous of you, Anthony," but "Ha," he roared, "I'll make her the finest horsewoman in Ireland."

A few years later, Anthony Lefroy "broke his neck in the hunting field, clean and swiftly, with no lingering humiliation of old age and sickness. His huge horse Centaur . . . crashed to his death with him." According to Helena, his will left instructions that he and Centaur should have a joint funeral:

> In another locality this might have dumbfounded the Rector but not in the north of Ireland . . . where our man of God was still of the Established Irish Church and had hunted many a mile and over thousands of fences with Uncle Anthony.
>
> To the discord of the village band, rendering Chopin's "Funeral March," Uncle Anthony carried high on his black-plumed catafalque, and dressed in the full regalia of hunting pink, wound down the drive of Carriglass Manor for the last time. Behind him on a gun caisson lay Centaur, draped in the colors of the Louth Hounds, saddle and bridle laid on top.... The hounds walked sedately, heads hanging, into the churchyard, where they waited decorously packed until the service inside the church was over, and the Rector came outside and preached the most beautiful funeral oration over Centaur I have ever heard before or since. When it was all over the Whip raised his bugle to his lips and sounded the "all away" and with bell-like cries they streaked out and over the churchyard wall, across the brown fields and through the woods, calling to a great figure in scarlet on a swift black horse, unseen by mortal eye.

I was sorry to discover that Uncle Anthony was actually buried in Dublin.

•

During the rest of the year in Richmond, Miss Gussie Daniel conducted Helena's formal education, but it was her grandfather's evening reading aloud that fed her fascination with words. He stopped occasionally to point out a Latin or Greek root; even as a small child Helena always asked of an unfamiliar word, "But what is its woot?"

Helena's weekly immersion in the rotundities of the King James Bible and the Book of Common Prayer also shaped her sentences; Minna Lefroy's gift to her niece, in 1912, of a New Testament was worn almost to rags by the end of Helena's life.

From her reading of Scripture as well as of Sir Walter Scott and the Romantic poets, her vocabulary grew large, and her phrases, whether written or spoken, went trippingly, but between her immersion in the romantic ideal of chivalry and her love of the Bishop's expedient lie to the pretty woman, Helena's grasp of truth was often ground fine. In contrast to her mother, Helena grew comfortable with handling a few grim details in service to a good story—but, like Sallie, she never questioned the social system that cocooned her.

Unlike Ellen Glasgow, her slightly older contemporary and neighbor, Helena never believed the South needed "blood and irony." Helena defended, throughout her life, the tenets of the South's belief in inherent aristocratic and racial supremacy, and these beliefs hobbled her writing.

Helena's girlhood was brief. When she was eighteen, she married Clifford Randolph Caperton of Wyndridge, near Union, West Virginia.

Clifford had come to Richmond in 1893 to pursue a career in business. A good-looking bachelor from a well-known West Virginia family, Clifford would have been invited to all the Richmond parties, including those in the Montagues' double parlor on East Franklin Street. According to a newspaper account, he became "thoroughly identified with the fashionable life of the city." He would have had many opportunities to meet Helena although she never described the courtship, which may have been brief.

Their 1897 wedding took place in the Montague parlor and was fulsomely described in the *Richmond Times-Dispatch*. "One of the most charming girls of the younger set," as well as a beautiful dancer and accomplished piano player, Helena was described as the granddaughter of the Very Reverend Jeffry Lefroy, Dean of "Jeremy Taylor's old cathedral, Dromore, County Down" and as the granddaughter of the Lord Chief Justice of Ireland. (She was actually his great-granddaughter.) Lady Helena Trent Lefroy was trotted out as another notable ancestor, although the veil sent over from Ireland for later family brides had not yet made its appearance; young Helena wore a tulle veil flowing from a diamond crescent—a creation that showed up in her later fairy tales. None of her Irish relatives attended.

"The house was decorated in faultless taste," the *Times-Dispatch* reported, "a blending of the green of delicate ferns, smilax"—that lost

Helena Trench Lefroy Caperton   *Clifford R. Caperton with two daughters*

staple of Southern festivities, cheap because plentiful in every back yard—"and palms, with the pure white of roses and chrysanthemums."

A flock of attendants—four children and ten adults, many of them cousins—wore white, while the older women—Sallie, Melinda, and Clifford's mother, Rosa Caperton—were smothered in black, somewhat lightened by "diamonds, old lace, dull jet and violets."

The long description hints, unintentionally, at the claustrophobic atmosphere in the crowded parlor, especially in Richmond's early summer heat.

In the studio portrait taken at the time of her wedding, eighteen-year-old Helena looks young for her age, pale, even a little sad. Her long, oval face is soft, unmolded. Her dark hair is drawn back in a chignon supporting an explosion of white. Her white peau de soie skirt with its short court train is cinched to the requisite eighteen-inch waist; the pointed toe of one white satin slipper ("tiny") peaks out. The two-piece outfit looks as though it might have been homemade in imitation of a popular period style.

Of her many portraits, this one looks the most uncertain, expressing nothing more than the patience the long sitting required. Patience will become, over the course of her difficult life, her most needed and most lacking quality.

She probably became pregnant on her honeymoon.

The *Virginia Times-Dispatch* does not tell where the honeymoon took place, only that the couple left on a train "for the North," with Helena wearing "a handsome navy blue tailored suit with cerise lining"—a color that will crop up in her later stories, as the lining of princesses' shoes.

She and Clifford spent part of their honeymoon at his family's ancestral home, Wyndridge, a large two-story house built in the late eighteenhundreds by William Gaston Caperton. The house still sits on 150 acres, surrounded by nine outbuildings, one the original settlers' cabin.

Tiny Union, West Virginia—its population today is less than six hundred—was given its name because it was a rendezvous for troops during the Indian Wars. It sits in the Allegany Mountains near the state's eastern border.

Originally part of Virginia, the mountain counties resented the Tidewater's dominance of the legislature. In 1861, the mountain region refused to support Virginia's secession and was recognized by Lincoln as a separate state in 1863.

Wyndridge was a working farm for three generations of Capertons, but they did not lack for education and refinement. Helena's new sister-in-law, Rose, was described in a magazine account as "a woman ahead of her time in the early twentieth century, a liberated woman who could run a farm well and raised blooded livestock, but could still retain the cultivated and refined manners of a nineteenth-century woman that had been instilled in her by her mother." Rosa Caperton, who "spent her days playing her Baltimore rosewood piano and attending the elegant formal garden."

But there was another side to Rosa Caperton, which Helena must have recognized with surprise. Her mother-in-law was credited with the early education of Matthew Clair, born in 1865 at Wyndridge, the son of slaves. He became the first black bishop of the Methodist Church and was sent to Nigeria to establish a church there.

According to her daughter Rose, Rosa "took great comfort in later life that Matthew Clair, a man of God, had risen so far."

This is the only indication that Clifford Caperton may have been raised in a slightly different atmosphere from the one that reigned on East Franklin Street.

Helena never used her Caperton in-laws as models for her fictional characters or as material for her essays. Instead she mined her own rapidly commencing life as the hard-pressed mother of seven children, writing two separate essays on the challenges of "barring the stork from the window and the wolf from the door"—not always successfully.

Her children were born so close together that two rode in the baby carriage at the same time. "Mother uses us for twins," these paired little girls told strangers. Birth control, their mother wrote, was both unmentionable and illegal, as was abortion. The eighth infant died two days after her birth, a blessing, according to Helena's essay; the big family was barely able to keep afloat.

Times soon became desperate for Helena, who dreamed of immersing herself in better things than the ordeal of raising six daughters and a son with only the help of one hired woman. Her grandmother Melinda had relied on three African-American nursemaids to care for her own children.

In two essays on raising her daughters, Helena outlines her child-rearing philosophy:

> Both my husband and I were raised in leisurely Southern homes. My life had been divided between Virginia and the North of Ireland. The combination is a goodly heritage, and so I determined to give my children all the best I had learned and absorbed from these so widely divergent homes.

She doesn't define their divergence; perhaps she only meant the geographical divide, or possibly something more elusive: an attitude or point of view that could explain a difference between the West Virginia Capertons and the Richmond Montagues. She skipped over entirely any ethos her husband introduced into the family.

I found a clue to Clifford Caperton's character in a pair of unsigned, unaddressed notes in the blue box. "He was a complete nonentity," someone, perhaps a Richmond acquaintance, observed. But another unnamed person countered, "[H]is full, useful, kind and active life was snuffed out so suddenly and needlessly in one cruel second." How these notes came to join the mementos in the blue box is unclear; in any case, Helena must have deemed them insightful enough to save.

Yet it is hardly enough to dismiss Clifford as a complete nonentity, especially because anonymity for the first notewriter has allowed for a degree of spite.

Certainly Clifford's birth was welcomed by his family. His grandmother, Caroline Clifford Stiles, wrote upon this occasion:

> Dear little man, Having heard of your arrival a few days ago I thought perhaps you might be interested in knowing that you have some relatives in the faraway north [she wrote to his parents in West Virginia from Connecticut] who are very much interested in your welfare. I shall always consider you my boy, so you must be careful and behave yourself, sir. . . . I have not yet engaged a room in college for you as I thought such an aged gentleman as yourself might prefer expressing an opinion in regard to which of the buildings you would wish to be in.

About the college itself there was no question: it should be Yale.

As a further indication of Clifford's character and of the expectations with which he was burdened, I have the letters he wrote to his parents, a large packet, fortunately preserved in my mother's blue box.

Dated variously between the fall of 1888 and the early summer of 1889, written while eleven-year-old Clifford was boarding with his Uncle Frank Newton at a school in New Haven where his uncle taught, the letters show that standards of penmanship, as well as spelling, had already begun their steep decline.

"You just ought to see my room it is a network of strings," he bragged. "There is one to pull my gas out without getting out of bed, one to pull my curtain up in the morning one to Aunt's room to ring a bell in my room and a place to put my Bible and dumb bells."

But in October, Clifford wrote mournfully, "I get offel homesick sometimes. We have not had but one or two pretty days since you [his parents] left."

He cheered up considerably later in the fall: "Uncle Frank found a bicicle over at the campus but it was too large for me and I am going to try to sell it. I am going to give up all my Christmas and get the Amatelle bicicle which they will sell for $10."

School routine was spiced with adventures: "Bernie and I got tickets and went down to Milfred (Milford?) on the train for chestnuts Friday." His aunt had mentioned a trip to New York to see Buffalo Bill's Wild West Show—which Sallie Montague Lefroy enjoyed in Richmond—but the trip did not happen.

He made up for this disappointment with other shows, writing home to say, "I went to see a woman whistle.... The woman whistled wonderfully. I wish you could have heard her."

On another expedition, he enjoyed "the educated horses they are the most wonderful things I ever saw one is a mathematician the man would say how much is 6+5 and the horse would paw 11 with her foot . . . but could not go over 48."

He began to sign himself "Jack Sharp," perhaps an adventuresome boy's shortsighted reference to Jack the Ripper, active in London in 1888.

By the spring, he'd managed to get an air gun and, in letters home, listed the number of sparrows he'd killed. In his childish, tear-along English, he reported that during morning prayers one got in the chapel "and chirped as loud as he could and I was just thinking if it would be disrespectful to commit murder on a sparrow with my gun in church."

He dissected one of his murdered sparrow's skulls, found its vocal cords and examined a cross-section of its heart. He treated these dissections as careful experiments, and thoughtfully included a diagram in a letter home.

His lively curiosity impelled him, once, to go "rather close to a coal hole where the steam was just pouring out, to look in, when a police-man got me by the collar and told me to get out and you can believe I scooted."

By the spring, Clifford was receiving top grades in all his subjects— arithmetic, language, geography, history and even spelling, but his attention was suddenly gripped by the notion of owning a crow. He wrote his father with explicit bartering instructions.

> Please tell Jim Hickum . . . or any other fellows that will do it, if he will get me a young crow and keep it until I come I will give him 50 cents for it if he says he won't do it for 50 cents tell him I give him 75 cents but (don't) tell him until he says he won't do it for 50 cents.

His signature was now a big flowing "Jack" angling down the page.

Clifford's after-school activities during his year away from home included fishing, swimming, rowing, ice skating, kite flying, making a thirty-foot canoe as well as a rowboat, collecting stamps, shooting birds, turtle hunting, owning white rats (and fish in a tin pan), buying and riding a bike for 150 miles, making a lamp for his mother, earning money by doing chores, and all this in addition to his schoolwork and the letters he wrote home, forty-seven in all.

No overscheduled eleven-year-old boy today can equal this, but the most striking difference from the modern fifth-grader's schedule may be that Clifford initiated all his extracurricular activities himself and carried them out either alone or with a friend. Although he was punctilious about asking his parents' permission via all these letters, he neither expected nor received any adult supervision—except from the occasional "police-man."

After Clifford went home to West Virginia in the summer of 1889 there are no more letters and almost no other record of his life;

he did not in the end attend Yale, which must have disappointed his grandmother. But if one grants the remote possibility of inherited characteristics, Clifford's stand out as a set that would bear repeating: inventive, cheerful, affectionate and conforming, happy and adventurous in childhood. Ultimately, however, he was less adapted to the demands of maturity, especially in the constricted Richmond society of his wife's family.

He married Helena not ten years after these letters were written. There are references to Clifford in some of his wife's humorous essays, but he seems to have had little relationship with his son, and his daughters were alienated by his attempts to involve himself in their lives, which they saw as interference.

He died in 1939, at the age of sixty-one, "from injuries received in an automobile accident" according to the obituary in a Richmond newspaper. By then, his son Arthur had been absent from his life for years and five of his six daughters had left home and gotten married.

The obituary outlines Clifford's career in general terms, noting that "Mr. Caperton had been engaged in the advertising business for a number of years. At the time of his death, he was district representative for the firm of Whitehead and Hoag of Newark, New Jersey." There is no list of honors, degrees, or club memberships, only the names of the six men who would carry his coffin.

His daughter Mary remembered at the end of her life that her father had been victimized by his wife's rage over his financial failures, adding that the advertising business in Clifford's time was still in its infancy and did not produce much money for anyone involved. But the firm of Whitehead and Hoag, established in 1890 with a capital of half a million dollars, had been a very successful business, employing several hundred people, selling advertising memorabilia in the form of tin trays and plaques with logos for beer, cigars, Turkish and Russian baths, and men's garters. As a traveling salesman for the firm through their Southern sales area, it seems that Clifford should have made a respectable living. Apparently he did not.

In a photograph taken in 1905, Clifford looks young, smooth and intent, with searching dark eyes and a handsome mustache half-covering his sensitive mouth; he holds two of his six daughters—perched on his knees in their frilly dresses, they look almost incidental. This handsome man in his spotless wing collar is looking beyond his little girls, beyond the photographer to some future opportunity, or excitement, which may never have arrived.

In her essays, Helena seems determined to take Clifford's shortcomings as a father and provider lightly. She even turned his inability to recognize his daughters' changing needs into an essay topic, trying to tame it with humor and cutting observation, as she did with so much unpleasantness. "It is a funny thing," she writes, "how fathers never realize their daughters are grown up."

To illustrate, Helena relates to her readers that "one of Father's ways of displaying how proud he was of his family was to take a guest up to the nursery and show him the row of little white beds with a golden head on each pillow."

This "indoor spectator sport" went on far too long. Finally, Helena reports, one adolescent daughter home from boarding school appealed to her

> with cries of indignation, "Mother, for goodness' sake stop father from showing us to people after we are in bed. . . . I just opened one eye to see a perfectly strange man in a dinner coat, having the beauties of the landscape pointed out to him by father, who was whispering something about 'little daughters.'"

In another essay, Helena makes light of his lack of awareness, describing Clifford's protest when one daughter was leaving to go out on a date. He complains to Helena, "She is entirely too young to begin this sort of thing. I am surprised you would allow it!" only to collapse crestfallen—"I should have been consulted"—when reminded that this daughter was three months older than his wife had been at their wedding.

"Of course," Helena consoles him, "she should have consulted you about growing up."

Helena circa 1930

Helena and Clifford's marriage had begun with high hopes. Helena writes that

> we considered ourselves only moderately well off. . . . We began housekeeping by putting a small legacy into a large and very inconvenient house. It was heated entirely by large open fireplaces, there were no electric lights, and only one bathroom. On the other hand, the rooms were lofty and flooded with sunshine.

As the babies began to arrive—Arthur, the eldest, was born in 1898—Helena writes in a later essay, "One very important handicap [was] vouchsafed in the game. We had servants . . . such as they were." The thirteenth amendment to the U.S. Constitution was long in place. These servants were paid, no longer slaves, but Helena continued to operate from the expectation that her life will have the same shape— loyal servants, a large house, an ample provider as a husband—as her mother's and grandmothers'. She writes:

> We had Mammy [Louise], to whom laws of modern hygiene were insults . . . Aunt Emma the cook, who went on periodic cocaine jags, and whom we dismissed regularly, and as regularly returned to cook breakfast the next morning, until the next outburst, which might require a squad of stalwart policemen and the city ambulance. Then there was that saint of God, Uncle Charles, who was supposed to do odd jobs when he didn't have misery in his back, and who waited table in a coat with Southern Railway on the collar, and who had "strokes" that required careful nursing.

After describing her eccentric household, Helena remarks, "No young woman can truthfully say she would choose seven babies in a corresponding number of years," even if each one had come "trailing clouds of glory." Like her mother's Richmond Woman's Club audiences, she knew her Wordsworth.

Much later, Mary, my mother, would recall that her mother finally went to her doctor, pleading for some form of birth control. Contraception was illegal because of the Comstock laws in effect since the 1870s; he'd had to tell her he could do nothing for her.

In her later essays, Helena began to deal more openly with the conflicts she felt as a girl too soon overwhelmed with responsibilities.

In one, "The Reward of Parenthood," written in response to an essay by "the despairing and exhausted young woman who so poignantly expressed herself in *Harper's*," Helena takes this complaining mother to task for having so many children:

> The first hostage to fortune perhaps, but after that you must have fully recognized what you were letting yourself in for, and that the cost of each child equals that of a yacht or a racing stable.
>
> Our boy came first, and my greatest regret is that he seemed by necessity turned over to the care of others because of the two little girls. He was eleven when the sixth little sister was two weeks old and we decided to send him away to school.

Her essay continues with a lament over her early child-rearing decisions: "I look back and my heart aches over my many mistakes" with Arthur, she continues. "The boy was honorable, he was to a certain extent an obedient boy, but O the things he did that it would never have occurred to me to forbid. He got too many whippings for one thing." These beatings stopped when he became too strong for his mother.

"I say unreservedly," she asserts, with the wisdom of hindsight, "that were I called upon to do the work of bringing up a family over again, I would not allow a blow to be struck." It seems likely that her daughters also felt the sting of the hairbrush, the slipper, or—worst of all—the belt.

In a studio portrait taken when he was about eight, Arthur's stance is defiant: his feet, in laced-up leather boots, widely spaced, a football clutched under his arm, his other hand on his hip. He stares challengingly at the camera.

Hoping for the best, Helena and Clifford sent him to "one of the finest church schools in this part of the country." While he was there,

Helena "lived in terror of his being sent home" because of his many escapades. Arthur's relative absence from the blue box—there is only one letter, a few photographs, and several news clippings—probably derived from her near-constant fear that he would get into trouble—again!—and embarrass everyone. Much later, according to family lore, his drinking would endanger his career as a commercial airline pilot and cause further dismay.

In 1917, when he was nineteen, Arthur sent a telegraph to his father, "Have joined up US Marine Aviation. Please do not interfere."

Helena with children Arthur and Rose

His determination, despite his drinking, kept him flying for the rest of his life. He first displayed it, according to a 1947 issue of the *Flagship News*, when he "ducked out and passed the age recorder's desk at the recruiting office and into the Navy during the First World War"—perhaps a bit of embroidery, since at nineteen he was old enough to join. But "boot camp wasn't a very promising place for a would-be flyer, so Art decided it was the Army that needed him.... A good number of manipulations and duplicate forms later, he was wearing khaki and learning to fly" in the Signal Corps, piloting "the crates which later day airmen claimed were made with baling wire and chewing gum."

Helena must have been anxious about his survival in wartime. Her uncle, George Lefroy, wrote reassuringly from The Palace, Calcutta,

"You must not worry about dear Arthur. He is in the hands of one who loves him as even you cannot do," adding, "It is splendid that you have been able to give a son to the great cause." (Military service was a Lefroy tradition; eleven men in the extended family served in World War I, two of whom died in action.)

Though he lived until 1954, very little is preserved of Arthur—Helena's only son—in Helena's portion of the blue box. Beyond the newspaper clippings and the sole photograph of his youth, the one letter Helena did keep was the letter he wrote his father Clifford in May 1927 after escorting Charles Lindbergh's airplane on the first leg of his solo flight across the Atlantic:

> I flew alongside of him, my photographer shooting pictures as fast as he could.... Lindbergh waved to us and I got closer hoping to get near enough to get his head in the picture.... I had a racing job that could sit right on Lindbergh's tail.
>
> Just as we were crossing the Sound about opposite New London, my motor started to act up.... I would have continued to Boston if I had had any other ship, but this racer lands at 75 per and you can't set her down in a cornfield. . . . I hated to do it, but better judgment told me to bat it back home before she pooped out on me entirely....
>
> Well, you know the rest: how he got to Paris and is the idol of the world. Don't let any wisecrackers tell you that he did not prove anything and that it was only a foolhardy stunt to get publicity. I know this guy and he is real and I don't know of a single airman who had the guts to try what he did. He showed that the earth-inductor compass is mathematically without errors and that dead-reckoning navigation is not only feasible, but entirely accurate enough for transoceanic flying.

This appears to have been the high point of Arthur's career, which had not lacked for other memorable moments: according to his account in the *Flagship News*, he flew the Andes and mapped China routes in World War I, later ferrying well-off New Yorkers from moorings in the Hudson River to Atlantic City, Southampton, Miami, and Key West in converted Navy bombers that "skimmed the treetops at a fast 90-mile-an-hour clip."

In 1923, he flew as a pilot for Gulf Coast Airlines, carrying mail from American "banana ships" landing at the mouth of the Mississippi River. His underpowered plane was often overloaded, and to get it off he ground, he rather improbably used the slick muddy swamp at the edge of the river: "Here flying speed could be accelerated more easily, and huffing and puffing, the plane would eventually become air-borne."

He then flew for seventeen years as a pilot for American Airlines, accumulating 3,000,000 air miles before retiring in 1949, according to the final news clipping that Helena saved.

Helena was surely amused by his accounts of his earlier days as a pilot when he flew Theda Bara to Atlantic City in an open plane through a dust storm that destroyed her makeup.

With his American Airlines captain's hat and pencil moustache, Arthur Caperton might have passed for a musical comedy lead, a role improved upon by his lighthearted adventures. He married four times and apparently had no children. Yet he seems to have made little impression on his sisters beyond serving as a cautionary tale, thanks to his alcoholism; perhaps his grandmother Sallie was better able to appreciate him, since she took her first airplane ride in his plane, causing an elderly relative to scold, "Silly old woman!"

•

After Arthur and his three younger sisters, three more girls were born, the last in 1910. By now Helena had invented her own labor-saving method:

> It became imperative after all six had arrived that I make a virtue of necessity, and enlist the aid of the three older sisters in bringing up the three younger. . . .
>
> If her baby had transgressed, she (the mother-sister) was called into consultation. When there was cause to be proud she was given credit for all accomplishments . . . it was a good way to save myself trouble . . . also it taught self-reliance and unselfishness.

Every spring and fall, the three older sisters shopped for their charges: "the most practical good sense was always shown by the little girls, to say nothing of good taste." Once the material was selected, the family hired an African-American woman to construct the girls' new dresses. According to Helena, they all looked forward to the days when this "seamstress would come to us, and there would be fascinating consultations over Junior Vogue and paper patterns, while the whirr of the sewing machine was heard in the land," stitching together "six times fourteen of everything. . . . Two hundred and fifty two garments in all. . . . Seven to wear, seven to wash," for each of the six girls.

Because the clothes were handed down from sister to sister, "the youngest sister never knew what it was to wear an entirely new coat till her fourteenth birthday."

At least one girl rebelled: my mother, Mary, showed her mettle early. When "a brown velvet coat that had never been popular" was passed down to her, Mary, "never one to sit down under affliction," as her mother said, went to Helena and, "looking me straight in the eye, said, 'The Salvation Army called today, Mother. I gave him the brown velvet coat. I just knew it would make you so happy to think it was keeping some poor little child warm.'" For once, Helena was at a loss for words.

In her essay, however, she demands the last word, noting piously,

> This sharing and passing along was never regarded as a hardship. If the older children in a family are brought up, line upon line, precept upon precept, there will be little trouble with the rest of them. . . . If in the family certain things "are not done," it has more weight than any amount of punishment.

Admitting that this form of discipline might hinder the development of a child's character, she writes, "Unless this individuality is founded upon implicit obedience, and an undeviating regard for the truth . . . no good roots can strike very deep." Helena's belief in roots, like her belief in avoiding things that "are not done," was also a family trait.

With six growing girls crowded together, Helena needed to believe that "it is the constant friction of a large family that wears down what is unworthy, and polishes that which is strong and fine," preparing children for "the battle of life." The participants in that battle, however, may well remember only the endless stress.

Around 1913 the family moved from inside Richmond's city limits to Westhampton. There, Clifford built a large, square, shingled house with ominous porticoes on a raw piece of land. Some of the money may have come from Sallie, whose portion of Dean Lefroy's estate now went largely to support her daughter and grandchildren.

While they were in Westhampton, one of the sisters, little Helena, showed signs of rebellion, running away half a mile to the streetcar stop because she felt she had been unjustly treated. Retrieved, she was sent to her grandmother. Sallie urged her to be more forgiving of her mother, who was pregnant again—with her eighth child, who would not live even two days past birth—very tired "and on the stress" and who had perhaps treated the little girl too harshly. Little Helena's response is not recorded. Years later, Mary cited this episode as an example of Sallie's influence as a family arbiter whose sense of fairness, as well as her appeals for compassion, soothed the little girls' rebellion.

Although Mary said in an oral history given in the last years of her life that her grandmother Sallie was "quite prosperous—her husband was, you know, Jeffry [sic] Arthur Lefroy,—in the end she was more or less impoverished because she had assumed so much of the expense of the growing family [Helena's]." Mary remembered that her grandmother, attending each granddaughter's birth, "would wring her hands and say, 'Oh my dear, where are we going to get the lace drawers and petticoats for these little girls?'"

Mary did not remember much about their childhood nurse, Louise, except for a single story that served as monument to Louise's creative problem-solving on behalf of her charges. In summers, when Mary and her sisters were small, Louise

> devised a plan to cool us off where she would put us in our nightdresses and we would take the open streetcar which had benches across and line us up on the first one where the great breezes were and off we would set to make the loop which went up Monroe Avenue. . . . Most people thought it weird to see all those little girls in their nightgowns.

Mary and her older sister Sarah devised another method of dealing with Richmond's hottest days: staying submerged in a bathtub of cool water, with the faucet adding more as the water warmed, they would lie reading their books, much to their grandmother's amusement.

Sallie preserved for her grown granddaughters a description of another of their escapades: during a family picnic, all the children except for the newest baby disappeared and were found hours later in a cave. Sallie sweetened everyone's anxiety by claiming that one child said she was glad the baby was not involved since she would have provided solace if none of the rest came back.

The girls' ethical education began early, taking place at home and in church, though only at the service itself since Helena had a horror of Sunday schools. "I do not claim that we were a deeply religious family," she writes, "but I saw to it that from earliest infancy, they were made familiar with the Books of the Bible."

No responsible mother, she believed, could raise her children without those biblical precepts, adding,

> I believe that [children] come to us perfect, "Even as our Father in Heaven is perfect." Completely perfect in every smallest braincell and nerve, and in their reaction to right and wrong. It is we who jangle those sweet bells out of tune by allowing fear to enter in. Fear is at the bottom of all wrongdoing.

She taught her girls that "no matter what you have done if you confess it fully and truthfully you will not be punished."

As the girls grew older, she occasionally read them contemporary bestsellers, even venturing into popular romances such as E. M. Hull's *The Sheik*. But she remained scornful of any book she felt was badly written; the sonorities of the King James Bible and Victorian writers such as Thackeray and Tennyson set her gold standard.

After about four years in Westhampton, the Capertons moved back to Richmond and Clifford bought a house in a new neighborhood at some distance from East Franklin Street. There the six girls were raised, and there Helena spent the rest of her life, struggling, at times, to pay the mortgage.

Fifteen Ten West Avenue is still a trim, attractive three-story house; it sports an enormous magnolia tree in its minuscule backyard. The Fan, as the neighborhood came to be called, was built at the end of the nineteenth century for the families of professional men. It had—and still has—an air of modest comfort, respectability, and charm.

West Avenue, a pretty little street with closely packed small houses, is now shouldered by the massive brick buildings of Virginia Commonwealth University. Dooryards with blooming jonquils and grape hyacinths, tiny porches, and façades painted more brightly than they would have been fifty years ago communicate a quiet air of domesticity. The neighborhood has always been full of children; Helena reminisced years later about being asked to "watch" little boys as they crossed the street, a service all the mothers provided.

Both of the Caperton family's moves may have been motivated by Miss Jenny Ellett whose girls' school, later to become St. Catherine's, moved at the same times from Richmond to Westhampton and then back again. All Helena's daughters attended school, at least briefly, with Miss Jenny.

An inspired teacher of the classics, Miss Jenny fired at least one of the Caperton girls with a love of learning. My mother, Mary, always credited Miss Ellett and another mentor, Louise Burleigh, with motivating her to apply for a scholarship to Radcliffe in 1924. Mary became the first woman in her family to graduate from college; her sisters completed their secondary education at Miss Jenny's or at boarding school.

By the time the family returned to Richmond, the older Caperton girls were nearly grown. Rose, the eldest, married at eighteen; her husband was not entirely to the family's liking. Two other sisters were old enough to be presented at the Richmond German and to partake of the year of pleasure their mother allotted them before the serious business of life began. The expenses of those debut years—dresses, flowers, food, parties—must have been difficult for the family, but the ritual was essential; Helena would never have considered allowing them to forgo it.

In the cramped West Avenue house strife was inevitable; Helena did not discourage it, believing strife and compromise valuable parts of the hardening process. The sisters did not always agree. One, asked to entertain another sister's unwanted boyfriend, replied that she had always worn her elder's castoff clothes but she refused to accept her castoff beaux.

"There was never anything in the icebox but flowers," Mary joked years later. Prospective suitors had kept it filled.

Helena used the constant presence of suitors as a topic for an illuminating essay wherein she explained how she dealt with "the boy question" in such a way as to avoid "the blood-curdling experiences so talked of and written about the modern young woman" who was beginning to bob her hair, shorten her skirts, and frequent speakeasies.

First, she always made the girls' suitors welcome in the house on West Avenue. "If a young man has spent happy congenial hours in a girl's house, there grows up a brotherly feeling of protection," a sure damper to sexual improprieties.

Helena's second rule was "Never show that you are shocked," in order to encourage intimate revelations from the daughter in question, while recognizing that "no human soul ever discloses itself entirely to another."

Third, "I give them complete freedom of thought and action. They know I trust their good judgment," a statement immediately modified by her anecdote about one young man: "When I got my first look at him and shook his hand, I knew I would rather see her dead than become his wife," adding, "To let her guess this would of course be fatal. I tried to keep on smiling."

Her silent disapproval was contagious; the family dubbed this unwanted suitor "The Miasma," one sister saying frankly, "I think he's awful." Helena made inquiries and found that "the unfortunate boy was all but ruined with dissipation and too much money"—the only occasion when she considered the latter a handicap.

Advised to prevent this daughter from going to visit the suitor at his college, Helena took the wiser course and said nothing. That visit finished the relationship.

Another anecdote has Helena barring the door to a caller. When he asked what he had done wrong, she replied, "Nothing, but I don't know your people."

Helen needed a theory to both organize and justify her attempts at matchmaking triage. She discovered it, she wrote in another essay on parenting, when she was bewailing to a gentleman friend the difficulties of raising six daughters. He advised, "Consider them your most valuable asset."

Inspired, Helena realized that she should treat her daughters as high-priced stock—"Pretty Girls Preferred." Marrying well would pay the desired dividend.

First she safeguarded her investment by instructing each baby daughter, "You are the most beautiful thing in the world. Kiss me." She wanted to insure that, through the development of the girl's self-esteem, "the seed of fastidious selection and ambition [was] implanted from earliest infancy."

Next, the Caperton girls had to live in the right neighborhood. Clifford's pleas to move somewhere cheaper were rebuffed: "Loss of caste is the unpardonable sin against your child"—especially for a family whose intense respectability didn't obscure their lack of money.

To increase the potential trading value of shares, low-caste men must be driven away; their presence would inevitably depress the value of the offering and better-heeled bidders would disappear.

Another threat would be staved off by giving the girls "the facts of life from the tender frankness of their mother's teaching, and not from the lips of servants or licentious schoolmates."

Helena knew there were men who might "endanger the imperishable beauty of a girl's innocent youth. . . . It were better that the detractor had a millstone about the neck and that they were cast into the depths of the sea"—a joint drowning, presumably.

Helena understood that her investment was displayed to best advantage during the "year of pleasure" granted to each daughter after high school, its centerpiece their attendance at that year's Richmond German. This year of pleasure also forestalled those cases of "arrested development one sees in women in their forties. . . . They have not had their fling at the proper time, so they clutch at it while there is still a remnant of youth left to them."

Before the marriage deal was signed and sealed, each daughter must become at least partly self-supporting as a stenographer, secretary, librarian, "athletic dancer," or playground director—the extent of Helena's list of acceptable possibilities.

The eldest, Rose, was already married, but even she had a year of war work in Washington; at eighteen, Harriette left home to begin her dancing career in New York. Helena writes that two of her girls, Harriette and young Helena, working then as a playground director, were able to "clothe themselves and attend to all personal expenses from their salaries. They would be quite equal to being thrown upon their own resources" if their marriage value was not recognized, which seemed unlikely. They were all very pretty girls.

Helena's fourth daughter, Mary, was aiming higher. "She announced to a more or less inattentive family that she would try for a scholarship," Helena writes in that same essay. "She did, and got it. The Distant Work Scholarship for our little girl!" This scholarship was offered at that time by Radcliffe to girls living more than thirty miles from Boston. In another article, Helena explains that this daughter won the scholarship because she was petite, blond, and—true to her family's perception of the power of roots—"pure Aryan."

Of course Mary too would marry, Helena believed; the tradition in their family was of long-lived widows or long-married wives, not of what Richmond's high society would have called Old Maids, the ultimate devaluation of Pretty Girls Preferred.

But even in the midst of the strenuous venture of seeing six daughters favorably married, Helena always managed to enjoy herself, especially when she gave "pink teas." As in Edwardian England, these parties featured pink candles, pink cakes, pink roses, and pink lemonade, as well as something higher proof, also pink.

These occasions impressed her daughters. On being told that she'd been born at four in the afternoon, one dutiful little girl sighed, "I hope it wasn't inconvenient."

Pleasure-loving Helena had reminded the woman who complained in *Harper's* that in her forties, after her children were raised:

> You will have earned the right to play as you wish, to take from life what it offers, and you will savor it as you never could without these years of deprivation and struggle. . . . Normally, you have just one youth, but with every daughter, another halcyon time comes to you. You live it all over in their joyousness. Together we have graduated, traveled, danced, seen the sun rise over the elms at New Haven after The Pump and Slipper or The Prom. Known June Week at Annapolis, in fact done all the thrilling, beautiful things that would only come once if one had no daughters.

What the daughters thought of this strenuous chaperonage was not recorded.

Though Helena was keen for all the delights that life could offer, she was never distracted from her essential labor: finding husbands for the five remaining unmarried daughters, husbands who would provide at least a glimpse of the golden apples of the Hesperides, especially as Clifford's income continued to fall.

In her view, her girls' only handicap was their "orchid tastes on zinnia pocketbooks."

Helena's training achieved the desired end: her daughters eventually married men of whom she approved both financially and socially, although the marriages were not always happy.

During the 1920s and '30s, Caperton debuts merged into Caperton weddings in a haze of white; the famous heirloom veil arrived, sent from Ireland by the Lefroys. It had been bestowed on Lady Helena Perceval, Arthur Lefroy's grandmother, by Queen Victoria when Lady Helena left her post as lady-in-waiting to marry. The veil's drooping lace folds would be worn, if not always prized, by several generations of brides.

The way to the altar was not always syrup-smooth. Mary's sister Sarah, so tiny she was sometimes mistaken for a child, fell in love with a man who died of a burst appendix during their engagement. Mary believed his family blamed Helena for not calling a doctor in time.

Sarah was heartbroken. She retreated to her room with the tiny dog her fiancé had given her. In 1928, Mary took her along on her trip to Greece; crossing the Atlantic, tiny Sarah sat on Mary's lap every evening, crying herself to sleep. Later, she married a persistent suitor Mary believed she never loved. Even after her marriage, Sarah kept a portrait of her dead fiancé on her dressing table.

Dying in 1961, a month after her mother, sad little Sarah was buried at Helena's side in Hollywood Cemetery. She was my godmother.

Of the six Caperton sisters there are two who held, at least for a time, significant ambitions. In 1924 Harriette, who had gone to New York with her dancing partner, Vernon Biddle, was spotted by a talent scout; according to family legend, the glamorous pair was strolling up Broadway. He offered them their first opportunity to begin a professional dancing career.

In a publicity photo, Harriette, sylphlike and soulful in white satin and chiffon, arches back against handsome Vernon. Her arms are outstretched, fingertips delicately extending her dress panels, one satin slipper exquisitely pointed. With her darkly lipsticked mouth and cap of short blond curls, Harriette is the embodiment of flapper-era romance.

Six Caperton Girls, circa 1922
(left to right): Melinda, Sarah, Helena, Harriette, Rose, Mary

Also in 1924, Mary entered Radcliffe College as a freshman.

A few years later, Mary scornfully declared that Harriette's partner wasn't really a Biddle. By then, she believed that her sister was having an affair, which tarnished her view of Harriette's dancing career.

Helena, however, was proud of both her enterprising daughters.

When Harriette danced at the Jefferson Hotel in Richmond (where the cornerstone, laid in 1897, contains commemorative notes, one written by Sallie), Helena was in the audience. Overhearing a woman remark that Harriette's bright blond hair couldn't be natural, she corrected the mistake tartly. Certainly it was natural! All her daughters were bright blondes.

•

In 1917, a new phase in Helena's life began: Rose's first child, Helena's first grandchild, was born when Helena was all of thirty-nine.

When the birth was imminent, Helena wrote in an unpublished article, she rushed to the hospital although Clifford warned her not to go, and found that he was right: Rose didn't need her or want her, attending to her newborn confidently, if casually, with the help of a hired nurse.

Helena described the visit with her usual jocularity. Her tone didn't quite conceal her confusion and hurt as she realized that her role as grandmother would be entirely different from her mother's. Sallie was crucial during every phase of her granddaughters' lives; Helena would hardly have survived without her.

But Helena's daughters all married well-off men; they were able to afford to hire plenty of help, escaping the need to call on their opinionated, sharp-tongued mother.

Although her daughters never needed her as intensely as she had needed Sallie, Helena was sometimes called in to help as her grandchildren grew older, especially when their parents wanted to travel.

She recalled one such experience in an unpublished article, probably written in the 1940s, called "In Loco Parentis."

Nothing could be more different, she explains, than the upbringing of the two sets of grandchildren she'd been asked to supervise during a summer vacation on Long Island. The first trio was "cloistered in the nurture and admonition of the Lord, with the blessings of otherwise unlimited wealth, with accompanying nannies, tutors, governesses . . . and alas of late, detectives."

The kidnapping and murder of Anne and Charles Lindbergh's baby in 1932 had caused panic among well-off parents, some of whom chose to hire around-the-clock detectives to protect their children.

Helena remembered that her "heart was wrung" when the eldest of the protected trio, David, was told by his "earnest young parents" to take a week to decide what he wanted for his eighth birthday. He announced immediately, "I want the day of my birthday to myself. Just the empty day for my own."

Helena writes that she had nearly cried out in anguish. Then she states firmly,

> I find myself constantly in league with my grandchildren, because I intend to have their entire adoration, and because I think certain whimsies of their young parents absurd. . . . I do not expect approval from my children's generation . . . but I will remain a Jesuit in this respect, for the end so often justifies the means.

Her declaration announced the onset of many struggles, but the outcome came to be what she hoped for: her grandchildren were by and large devoted to her.

In her article, she writes that as soon as the parents of the protected trio left, she realized, "I could transgress rules with pagan freedom." The other set of cousins was expected to arrive immediately: "No guard or anything?" one of the privileged trio asked. "So far as I know," Helena replied. "How wonderful," sighed an envious chorus.

The cousins arrived in a Model T Ford, which they had restored and painted "a rich shade of rose madder. They called it the Odalisque. It stood quaking in every joint, smoke pouring from the exhaust, with a noise that shattered heaven."

On the way to Long Island, the cousins from Virginia reported, they were stopped by a policeman and given a ticket "for our stink and our noise . . . but it's all right, we threw it away."

After "withdrawing behind the tea kettle" to avoid comment, Helena observed, "which of these systems used by my young parents will be the most successful the years to come will show."

Eighty years later, the outcome seems to favor the trio in the Odalisque. Of the privileged children, two died early and tragically, while the unsupervised trio have gone on to lead apparently normal lives.

Two of these six grandchildren were girls. Rapturously, Helena describes one granddaughter as having "very thick tangled-up black lashes . . . red mouth promis[ing] honesty toward love . . . hair in a pale gold mantle, which the girl detests." Her hyperbole echoes Sallie's encomiums of her friends' beauty seventy years earlier.

Something more than blond hair had passed from Helena to at least one of her grandchildren. This thirteen-year-old girl, "Tennysonian in her tall fairness," displayed "a ruthlessness of purpose. It doesn't do to get crosswise of Elaine."

Over the course of their Long Island stay, Helena discovered that Elaine had caused her governess "sudden and violent nausea" by dosing her secretly with ipecac so that the girl could go alone, "in purest white mousselaine de soie, tiny pearls and lily of the valley" to her "first late dance."

Helena might have disapproved of Elaine's method, but she appreciated her aim. And after all, as she herself noted, "the end so often justifies the means."

Earlier on that Long Island vacation, she anticipated trouble when "the waiting spark" brought by the enterprising cousins would set off an explosion among the three "groomed, guarded, and ceaselessly instructed." Helena might have been anxious but she was, as always, alive to adventure.

"So much being provided for their amusement, the first two or three days passed without noticeable incident" as Helena marveled at their diving—"lithe young bodies described a bright arc high above my head"—puzzled over the absence of "difference between my girls and my boys, clad as they all were in the briefest of rubber loin cloths," admired their tennis and riding, and especially as she admired the less-privileged cousins' willingness to learn from the protected trio's more polished athletic skills.

Their upbringing had already produced dramatically different results. The less-privileged cousins "browsed at will" in their parents' library. They understood a reference to "Smithfield" as suggesting Virginia's "peanut-fed hams" while their more traditionally educated cousins recognized "the smell of burning Bishops"—suggesting, to Helena, Queen Mary's persecution of the Protestant Church's most prominent members, one of whom, John Rogers, was burned at the stake in Smithfield in 1555.

Helena observed that the well-supervised trio thought *Vanity Fair* referred exclusively to a magazine: "Result, an hour with Mr. Thackeray every evening."

Helena's comparison is neat: information about British history and contemporary fashion on the one hand, local knowledge and the nineteenth-century classics on the other. It is easy to guess which Helena found more congenial; *Vanity Fair*'s Becky Sharp was one of her heroines, her power sanctified by her bad end.

All during the vacation, the protected trio was tailed by their detectives, "a source of fascination" to the other cousins but "boring adjuncts" to the children they guarded.

Helena admitted to a "sinking of the heart" at the sight of the detectives' "solid forms, with the ominous holsters" and "the small black car one drove behind us whenever we went off the place."

One day, "I set out to see what the children were doing and tell them to stop it." She found the six cousins in the garage, listening rapt while "the arm of the law tipped back in a chair against the wall was graphically regaling them with horrific incidents" from his previous employment in "The State Asylum for the Criminally Insane."

When Helena reprimanded them for listening, one of the privileged trio countered, "It's so terribly interesting, especially if you have read Havelock Ellis. Nearly all insanity has a basis in sex complex."

The remark seemed to prove their parents' liberality until it was revealed that the speaker had secretly ordered the Ellis books, while his apparently less-sophisticated cousins had free access to the same books in their parents' library.

Helena concluded comfortably, "The ardent mind of youth will pierce the heart of knowledge in its own irrevocable way."

Her grandchild's reference to Havelock Ellis presaged a tornado of change for Helena's family and for the world around them. Ellis's studies in the psychology of sex, published before the First World War in a set of seven volumes, caused an outburst of prudery; the first two volumes were banned. He dared to discuss aspects of human sexuality many late Victorians preferred to ignore, especially male homosexuality. Ellis also championed women's social, economic, and erotic rights. He understood that economic dependency, psychological repression, and erotic timidity all limited women's possibilities. His views, streaming through many channels, would eventually affect all of Helena's grandchildren, even the privileged set, once they escaped the guards.

More immediately, Helena's humorous mention of Havelock Ellis presaged the period when she would publish her two volumes of short stories, as well as many articles, trying diligently—always hating her typewriter—to restore her family's declining fortunes.

Helena Caperton set out to write short stories—or legends, as she called them—at the same time that her Richmond contemporaries, James Branch Cabell and Ellen Glasgow, were achieving much greater renown.

Glasgow believed her fiction would deliver a salutary dose of reality to the South; Helena had no such ambition. Her aim was to entertain. She never earned the respect of the literary world, as Glasgow did with her accomplished novels; Glasgow's *In This Our Life* won the Pulitzer Prize for Fiction in 1942.

Cabell had secured a reputation thanks to his ironic fantasy tales, admired by H. L. Mencken and Sinclair Lewis. His satirical novel *Jurgen*, published in 1919, led to a famous obscenity case, which he and his publisher ultimately won.

Helena viewed Cabell as a friend, which resulted in the preservation of her papers in the James Branch Cabell Library at Virginia Commonwealth University. She never mentioned Ellen Glasgow, an early supporter of suffrage who lectured at least once on the topic in Richmond.

But Helena did have some measure of literary success. One of her short stories was reprinted in the 1933 O. Henry Awards collection with, among others, "Smoke" by William Faulkner. But she was tormented by financial worries and only wrote what she believed would sell to the women's magazines of the 1940s and '50s.

In her short stories, Helena draws on the rich and often problematic vocabulary of nineteenth-century letter writing and sermonizing, on Curtie's Irish tales, on her childhood's myths about slavery and racial determinism, often using the rhythms of the King James Bible. Her articles resemble popular women's writing of the time, such as *Cheaper by the Dozen* or *Please Don't Eat the Daisies*, where the conflicts involved in raising large families become the stuff of jokes. At times her humor seems to muffle a scream of frustration.

She tried to be hard-working and determined, although Richmond social life and family obligations inevitably interfered. Her pursuit of fun—parties, clothes, and alcohol (a rumor had her giving her bootlegger a party on the eve of his imprisonment)—weakened her efforts. But in the midst of this chaos and distraction, Katherine Anne Porter commented on one of her collections, Dorothy Parker introduced another, and Helena's two books were reviewed widely and respectfully all over the South.

In her introduction to Helena's first collection, *Like a Falcon Flying*, published in 1943 by Garrett and Massie, Dorothy Parker wrote— with surprise amounting to alarm:

> These are curious tales to come from the pen of a gentle, pretty Richmond lady.... They are swift, tense, emotional.... But there is more, a fierce rush of drama, a long-spreading terror, a passionate championing of the lovely and the innocent and then a curious tenderness.

Lines from "The Falconer of God" by William Rose Benét preface the collection:

> I flung my soul into the air
> Like a falcon flying...

Of all Helena's stories, the one that still exerts the strongest spell is this collection's title story. In "Like a Falcon Flying," the main character, Zoe, does have certain falconlike characteristics, and her triumph in the end depends on her flinging her will if not her soul into the air. She is not, however, the falconer of God, but instead the falconer of erotic love.

The story is set in Ireland, Helena's father's country and the land of her childhood explorations. According to the flyleaf, Helena Lefroy Caperton was a great-niece of Dean of Westminster Richard Chevenix Trench, who published *On the Study of Words* in 1851. The book was originally a set of lectures Trench delivered. Helena would have agreed with him that in words, even when taken singly, "there are boundless stores of moral and historic truth, and no less of passion and imagination laid up."

But in "Like a Falcon Flying," Helena borrows her ancestor's elegant English for unexpected ends: "You are not obliged to kiss me at all, you know, but when you do, kiss me as though you mean it." Zoe's opening sentence owes much to Scarlett O'Hara, while retaining a tang of its own.

In her romantic fiction, Helena remains conscious of that sense of inherited privilege that is, for her and her family, bound up with their sense of history and of caste. Zoe and her long-time suitor, Diarmid, have the "indomitable air of race, and line, about them, that no hardship could ever erase," not even the poverty that is preventing their marriage.

Out riding, the pair, who have long loved "with the bitter chastity of the Celt," reach an impasse: Diarmid announces that he's going to marry an American heiress whose funds will save his decaying Castle Tandegree. Zoe rails at him, "You are willing to become her groom of the stables; you will allow her American dollars to buy you and all you stand for; how stupid, how blind you are."

Dismounting, Diarmid tries to excuse his actions with a claim that the heiress "always gets what she wants," at which, "with her booted foot, Zoe kicked him in the face" and rides off with a curse for the heiress: "I hope to God she breaks her neck."

Shortly after the marriage, the American does just that—she's no kind of rider. But instead of "loving, yet destroying each other," Diarmid and Zoe marry and settle into cozy domesticity in his castle, restored with the American's money.

Qualms of conscience are stilled by ritual, as are angry ghosts: "Every night at bedtime, when the good smoky Irish whiskey is brought, they stand and raise their glasses to her spirit" while "one of the many dogs will sense an unseen presence, and its hackles will rise stiffly, and it will gaze long into the dusty corners of the vast room."

Without quite intending it, Helena shows that a woman of will gets what she wants, by fair means or foul. Perhaps that's why this story was not included among the five earlier works that were reprinted in her second collection.

"Like a Falcon Flying",is the only story Helena sets in Ireland, and the only story in which she allows her main character to fly into a rage. Something about placing the action in Ireland, in contrast to Virginia, seems to have freed her, and the connection made on the flyleaf with Archbishop Trench contributed. That Helena claimed him as her authority released her, at least once, from a narrower self-definition.

If Helena, somehow escaping the chains of poverty and Southern gentility, had partaken of the wider education the Archbishop enjoyed, her native talent might have bloomed into imaginative daring. Zoe's wildness might have led Helena to some interesting places in her fiction, but she needed to make money, and gradually the wildness was tamed.

Inevitably, her Southern prejudices undermined her writing. She tried, ineffectively, to redeem one particularly embarrassing example, a story called "Nigger Foot," by retitling it "Negro Foot," but the perspectives of racial determinism and her own narrow-minded grasp of social privilege remained.

Her second collection, *Legends of Virginia*, published by Garrett & Massie in 1950, contains two stories that are superior to her earlier work in style and compression: "The Honest Wine Merchant" and "The Lost Governess."

Like several of her stories, "The Lost Governess" is told by an unnamed doctor who speaks with unquestioned authority. He describes a set of ambitious but impoverished parents of his acquaintance, "worn fine by five years of war."

These parents are distressed by their inability to pay for their three children's schooling, lamenting that "one generation without education, no matter what the birthright may be, and disintegration has set in." The two sons and the daughter must work as field hands to support the family, even though both boys are capable of intellectual development and the girl, Victoria, has an extraordinary voice, "a great gift."

One stormy night—that staple of Victorian fiction—when the parents are bewailing their poverty, a stranger knocks at the door, clearly "a gentlewoman" although rain-soaked and near collapse. Her refined face shows "the pallor of long confinement."

The family takes her in. When she sees their library, she exclaims, "Books!" revealing a passion that impresses the parents. There begins a "beautiful association" as she enters the family as an unpaid governess, brings the boys' education up to scratch, and gives Victoria singing lessons.

Then, suddenly, after some months, she disappears—"gone without trace"—leaving her pupils imbued with "the uses of learning"; interestingly, not the love of learning.

The doctor later visits the state insane asylum and hears a voice singing, "Sweet amaryllis, by spring's sweet tide"—a song the governess taught Victoria. He insists on being admitted to the cell, although the superintendent warns him that the inmate is violent, especially with men.

There he finds the lost governess raving, wearing a straitjacket, which he orders removed. She attacks him, trying to scratch out his eyes. Straitjacketed again, she lapses into incoherent mumbling, while the superintendent explains that she has been closed up for years, only once escaping for a few months. When she came back, of her own free will, she said she was afraid she was about to begin, again, to inflict harm.

This story recalls both Charlotte Brontë's *Jane Eyre* and Helena's childhood visits to the poorhouse's mental patients, but she didn't credit either with inspiring this tale. Lecturing on her stories at the Richmond Woman's Club, Helena revealed to her audience that

> "The Lost Governess" happened in one of those houses situated upon the banks of the James River. Four blackened chimneys are all that mark the spot today. I was told the story by a very old lady who, in her childhood, had known the Doctor's family.

Helena preferred the authority not just of a doctor's voice but also of a seemingly actual historical event.

"The Honest Wine Merchant," from the same collection, shows Helena's potential advance toward abstraction, an impulse that is reminiscent of Isak Dinesen.

Here, the characters have neither names nor descriptions; they are simply The Honest Wine Merchant, The Young Doctor, The Young Colonel, and The Lawyer. The point of view is detached; the setting stirs "the chords of memory" but is not specified, other than being the cellar of the Wine Merchant whose work is "a sacred calling."

He invites some friends to drink a rare Madeira from a cask, just arrived, that has been "twice around Cape Horn." As they drink the wine, two of the men discover golden hairs, one on his sleeve, the other in his cup. These men persuade the merchant to descend into the cellar, by dead of night, with a terrified slave who is ordered to hack open the cask. As the Madeira runs out, the men see more blond hair streaming and, finally, a perfectly preserved naked woman of great beauty.

"Some act of love and violence," they guess, placed her there a hundred years earlier. From that day on, the men "shrank from . . . [yet] yearned toward" golden hair and Madeira wine.

"'The Honest Wine Merchant,'" Helena told her Woman's Club audience, "has had a most unexpected career. My grandfather was the Young Colonel and took part exactly as the story describes him." The title she gives John Henry Montague is surprising since he never served in the Civil War. Not satisfied with the limits of fiction even once it was completed, Helena could not resist the snap of a good story, and so she asserts that the stories she created were not merely imagined, but had extensive basis in fact.

Her tales, she told her audience in this same lecture,

> take place in all communities: stories that live evanescently among contemporaneous happenings as gossip, or, sadly enough, as cruel scandal. The passing of time often softens judgment, and enables us to regard these events in the abstract until they become folklore worthy of transcription.

For her second collection, *Legends of Virginia,* she moved into writing what she called "folklore"—legends that place her stories comfortably in an idealized past. Legends—in this sense—were what Helena believed her readers expected, and it was what she knew how to write.

Her stories are often surprising, if for nothing other than their melodrama, and for their unvarying adherence to codes of behavior used to keep each caste in its place, even as more complex ideas about freedom and equality were beginning to gather steam throughout the 1940s and '50s. They are frequently hard to bear, as is "Miss Angel Gabriel," for example.

This story's young African-American protagonist falls in love with a beautiful white girl whom he has seen half undressed when his mother, a seamstress, is fitting her ballgown. At first he imagines she is an angel—"Miss Angel Gabriel." Later, seeing her in a Harlem nightclub being pawed at by a group of white men, Helena writes, "his negroid maleness rose up" at the sight of her white seducers. They murder him for trying to defend her, exercising what they and the author believe to be their "rightful supremacy . . . inalienable right." The story is told from the young man's point of view, which establishes some sympathy for him, but the righteousness of his murderers is never questioned.

This is the story that inspired William Rose Benét to write Helena in 1943, "You have the true story teller's gift." After receiving praise such as this, Helena had even less motivation to move beyond the cruel tropes of the American South's racial obsessions.

Helena's fictional white women, although frequently victimized by poverty, sometimes fight their way up, and they—unlike their black counterparts—rarely bear the brunt of punishment; an example of this sort of heroine can be seen in "The Primrose Path of Dear Papa."

In this story, an impoverished seamstress, Miss Pocahontas, "lived in a sad locality," tyrannized by her mother who worships the memory of her philandering husband. After her mother dies, Miss Pocahontas receives 150,000 dollars—"a great restorative"—which is the remainder of the guilt money her father was forced to pay years earlier for having seduced a married woman.

The omniscient narrator tells the reader:

> I never believed in the theory that people who have been poor
> do not know what to do with money when they get it. Miss
> Pocahontas did. She sold that awful house. . . . Then she went

to the best dentist in town, and had all her teeth out and a perfect set made. It lifted the lines of her face. Then she went to Florida, and soaked herself in sunshine. She always had a certain lean flair.

And so, attractive and solvent, Miss Pocahontas is now set for a successful life, especially since she never inquires into the source of her windfall and so is able to preserve her faith in her "sainted father."

Helena's writing could never have made more than pin money, and her situation became dire after Clifford's death. Rose was by then divorced and remarried, but other daughters' marriages suffered crises, and Helena's sons-in-law were neither as rich nor as obliging as she had expected. She was cumbered with the mortgage on the West Avenue house, with no income other than small checks from her writing and Clifford's ten-thousand-dollar insurance policy. By now her portion of Dean Lefroy's estate was exhausted, and Sallie, with her own resources used up, had come to live with her.

Something more was needed.

Knowing Richmond society from the inside, Helena put together *A Record and History of the Richmond German, 1866–1939/40*, following it with a volume called *The Social Record of Virginia*, both apparently self-published.

The introduction to the latter was written by a relative through her daughter Melinda's marriage, Rosewell Page. Page states authoritatively, "It is always the aristocrat who recovers most swiftly from adversity," which could have been Helena's motto. He calls Virginia society the summation of culture, defined by Matthew Arnold as "knowing the best that has been thought and said in the world." Page goes on to endorse the practice of slavery, because, he writes, it enabled the writing of Poe's "The Gold Bug," Thomas Nelson Page's "Marse Chan," and Joel

Chandler Harris's Uncle Remus stories, perhaps the only time minor works of fiction have been used to justify human bondage.

The Social Record contains more than two hundred pages of the names of those Helena would have considered "First Families of Virginia." She indicated that the selection was made by committee; Richmond gossip held that she solicited names and printed them for a fee. The luster of this volume, dim at best, was considerably darkened by the imputation, true or not, that inclusion was bought.

But there were other successes. She acquired, in 1942, a respected New York agent, Elizabeth Oakes, who became her editor as well as her friend.

And of course there were her six daughters' marriages, all conducted with the usual pomp at Richmond's St. James Episcopal Church. In an article (the best-paid-for, she said, of all of them) called "The Care and Feeding of Sons-in-Law," she laid out her rules.

Although "so far there have been no mistakes" in her own six daughters' marriages, in this essay she offers solutions for disenchanted wives: a trip to the Derby (afterwards, the couple "came together like two shoe brushes"), a set of sables, a diamond bracelet, or a vacation in Bermuda. "Save the surface and you save all," she writes, and "agree with thine adversary speedily"—this last advice aimed at the disappointing husband rather than his fleeing wife.

But the decades had roared on, and sometimes more drastic solutions were needed. A grandson's pneumonia provided a lesson for his parents: "Those two wild goats with their dancing and card playing and running around."

"The Care and Feeding of Sons-in-Law" was followed by two more articles, all three of which, Helena said in a talk at the Richmond Woman's Club, sold quickly to the *Ladies' Home Journal* for three hundred dollars each, a substantial sum at the time.

"I was convinced that hitherto I had been an unsung genius," she told the ladies. But her fourth article was rejected with a form letter, the two editors who had accepted her earlier material having left the magazine (she believed she caused their dismissal), and, worst of all, she'd spent the anticipated check in advance.

But, she told her audience, "It was the best thing that ever happened to me, for it made me work hard, and humbly, which I had not done before. After that the family articles sold like hot cakes."

An article titled "The Strange Case of a Mother of Six Daughters," was also turned down, with a note (written, she said, by what must have been a sour old virgin) that criticized the author for failing to take her responsibilities seriously. As Helena told her audience, the labor of raising six daughters on little or nothing would have been unendurable without a sense of humor.

After that rejection, she had great difficulty selling anything.

Perhaps encouraged by Oakes, still her agent, to write something that would make more money than short stories, Helena embarked in the late 1940s on her first and only novel, originally titled *Unkept Vineyards*. She dedicated it to her daughter Mary and Mary's husband Barry Bingham and, in an act of bravado, sent the manuscript in 1951 to Mary for editing.

Set in the antebellum period, written for women readers of commercial fiction, *Unkept Vineyards* is an indigestible porridge of Southern myth, nostalgia, and racism, featuring a persecuted snow-white beauty, Mary Lee, of august lineage.

With her editor's blue pencil poised, Mary must have read the manuscript with misgivings. Well-educated, sophisticated, and passionate about correct usage, she would have guessed that she faced an impossible task: to correct her mother's prose without offending her.

Her first comment chides Helena for this overheated sentence:

"She could lift the moment's chalice and taste its sweetness." "A bad cliché," Mary writes, "and the whole sentence somewhat too Delphic and oracular for the moment. Would cut."

Mary can't bear such euphemisms as "olfactory organs," and the phrase "bevies of lovely girls" elicits a shriek in the margin: "Mother! How could you! This is quite awful, I think."

More calmly, she questions, "Does it strike you that Mary Lee quotes the New Testament to herself quite a lot? It makes her seem so sententious." When the heroine observes that her world "seems dissolving around her," Mary queries, "Does it strike you that her world seems dissolving around her a great deal?"

Maddened by the repetition of "dainty" as a necessary attribute of "sweet women," Mary writes, "The women are always sweet. Perhaps they really were, but I think you should cut this out as often as you can bear to do so."

In a weird scene, Mary Lee, mysteriously ill, is visited by a doctor, giving rise to a description of another sick lady so modest a hole had to be cut in a sheet so the doctor could examine her tongue. Here Mary remarks tartly, "In the original version, the sheet was cut not to expose the tongue but another part of the anatomy."

Helena may not have been dismayed by her daughter's criticism; she may even have appreciated that Mary took the manuscript seriously. In any event, she checked off only a few of her daughter's criticisms. When she revised the novel, renaming it *Then Falls Thy Shadow*, she relied on her own instinctive storytelling rather than Mary's corrections. The novel was never published, perhaps never even submitted, and its death marked the end of Helena's writing career.

Whether or not lack of success ended Helena's writing, one thing is clear: by the 1950s the financial goad had been blunted. Her daughters were all married, her son was working as an airline pilot, and eventually, one son-in-law came to her aid, paying off the mortgage on the West Avenue house. Helena kept the cancelled check, for $5,750, for the rest of her life.

During her later years, Helena circulated between her daughters' households, telling stories to her grandchildren and great-grandchildren, gaining weight and opinions, both abetted by her evening toddy. Displaying the exquisite needlework she may have learned from Curtie, she whipped lace onto party dresses for her granddaughters.

No one ever called Helena "grandmother." Her family name, "Munda," based on some child's attempt at a nickname, stood for her rapt and sometimes terrifying storytelling, her determination to have her say in all situations, and the powerful complications in her relationships with her daughters.

One of Helena's great-granddaughters, Helena Sliney—known in the family as Nini—described, in her unpublished memoir, her relationship with Helena: "I was Munda's favorite. There was never any doubt in my mind." Nini recalled observing Helena's breakfast ritual, noting that her grandmother was always fully dressed—this meant stout girdle, stockings and high heels—by the time her breakfast tray was delivered. Although she never seemed to eat, Nini remembered, she made a ceremony of pouring and stirring her coffee.

Nini watched with fascination as Helena dropped a tiny white pill into her cup—saccharine, which the little girl imagined was a magic pill that would allow her to live forever.

Helena's character was not softened by the passage of time. Her judgment, once delivered, was never modified. Even on her deathbed, she was swearing that a nephew who had displeased her would never become a lawyer in Richmond; after thirty years of trying, her prohibition somehow indeed prevented him from passing the bar. Until the end, she was a force to be reckoned with in Richmond, writing to the *Times-Dispatch* on November 7, 1951, to express her outrage at plans to build an expressway through the city.

Reviewing books for her son-in-law's Louisville newspaper, Helena's blind spots are glaring: she hates "the nightmare regions of Tennessee Williams and Faulkner," objects to a new biography of Dickens because "it throws frightening light on an author whom we have hitherto regarded as a fireside companion of mirth, warmth and peace," and praises Elizabeth Bowen primarily not for her writing but for her Irish background.

She paid old age no sentimental tributes: "When things refuse to die a natural death, we have a duty to help Nature."

As Helena aged, her long visits with her daughters may have been tolerated rather than enjoyed. According to a family myth, she suddenly erupted at a dinner party, exclaiming out of nowhere, "I don't care what you say, it's all sex!"—a belief borne out by her history and her fiction.

She commemorated a 1954 visit to her daughter Mary in Louisville with an article called "Captain Mary Green," published in both the *Richmond Times-Dispatch Magazine* and a London periodical. The article is an encomium to the only female riverboat captain on the Ohio River. Helena was most impressed by the captain's ladylike demeanor, her spotless boat—"Never was a house on land this clean!"—and her angel food cake, which precipitated her only moment away from the wheel, to snatch the cake from the oven.

Her storytelling gets the better of her when she describes the funeral of the captain's husband: how he lay in state in the prow of his ship as did the Vikings, and how this Captain, Wife, and Mother, had allowed no one to take the wheel. Thus, while the crowd upon the shore bared reverent heads, she brought him over the water to his last resting place.

The romanticism that doomed her writing to obscurity had a sharper claw in the racism she was never able to examine or soften. Here, as the riverboat is being unloaded, Helena notices the roustabouts, "black and gigantic as they plodded in a rhythmic circle from boat to levee moaning their chanties."

Helena would have been astonished to learn that, even before the Civil War, these riverside workers had usually been freed men, and retained the dignity of what was considered a good job. It never occurred to her that they existed outside of her own use of them as exotic artifacts, or as in so many of her stories, victims of melodramatic, primitive urges.

•

In the rare manuscript room at the James Branch Cabell Library at Virginia Commonwealth University, where Helena's papers are preserved with a respect that would delight her, the dagger I remember seeing in her curio cabinet in Richmond lies within the files. It rests inside a delicately tendrilled sheath with a broken-off end. Its handle is covered with hammered scales; its rounded top is ornamented with five silver bumps.

Helena told me when I was a child that the dagger played a role in "The Chinese Lady," a story from her second collection.

This story, set in 1854, is another of Helena's exotic stories in which a noble voyager from the civilized world is lured to doom by a primitive and sexualized culture. The story begins when a nameless young Virginian signs on as an officer on Commodore Matthew C. Perry's flagship, one of a fleet of fifteen vessels–the "black ships"–that left Hampton Roads, Virginia, and sailed around the world for China before going on to Japan.

In Hong Kong, Perry and his officers are invited to a banquet at the palace of a "High Mandarin." During the elaborate feast, where only men are present, the Virginian is fascinated by "dove-like sounds" from behind an ivory screen, and surmises that the ladies of the court are hidden there—their host's "Most Precious Possessions." As the Americans are leaving, a hand reaches out from behind the screen and snatches the Virginian's bandana. Next day, a messenger arrives at the flagship and gives the Virginian his bandana, which is covered on both sides with exquisite embroidered silk flowers. Somehow he interprets the embroidered message: he is to come to a certain gate, at midnight. There, he is greeted by a delicate maiden, just fifteen, who introduces him to what the author terms the "Art of the East . . . The Century Old Cult of Love."

On his last night, the Virginian returns to the gate. He is seized by soldiers, bound, and brought to the Mandarin's throne room, thronged with his silent courtiers. His lover is brought in, dressed in silver and white and all her jewels. She is stripped naked. Then the Mandarin descends from his throne, turns back his sleeves, and disembowels her with a silver dagger, which he thrusts, bloodied, into the Virginian's belt. The following day, the fleet sails with the Virginian below deck, having lost his mind from grief.

Back in Richmond, his family arranges a propitious marriage. He and his fiancée go to the old resort, White Sulphur Springs, and there she dares him to climb a tall pine. In doing so, he falls to his death.

Helena ends her tale, using again a final, punchy proof: "I have the dagger and the handkerchief." And she did.

I saw them both, years ago: a blue-and-white-checked cotton bandana, covered with intricate embroidery, and that sheathed dagger. Helena took them from the depths of her curio cabinet where she kept the objects that proved, to her mind, the validity of her legends.

The bandana fascinated me even more than the dagger. Why, I wondered at the time, waste so much artistry on such a homely object?

While writing her story, I've come to see that, with her stories and her essays, Helena embroidered the mundane reality of her life as the hard-pressed mother of seven, transforming its cheap cotton with rare silk flowers. Behind the embroidery, the poignard flashes—violence as a necessary ingredient of romance.

•

In 1958, when Helena wrote her will, she used it to impress on her many descendants the importance of their family history.

Two prized items Helena bequeathed were given to the family "by the royal household" when Helena's great-great-grandmother by marriage, Lady Helena Perceval, left Queen Victoria's court to marry Reverend Frederick Stewart Trench: the first, a diamond bow knot brooch from the Earl of Arden and Egmont; the second, the Limerick Point wedding veil Queen Victoria had ordered, made by the lacemakers of Limerick. With the veil's bequest, Helena launched a new family tradition: "It is my wish that as far as possible future brides in our family will wear this veil." Her family's past in Virginia was commemorated by a gift of "the old slave chest in the front hall."

Finally, bequeathing "the ancestor engravings that hang in the front hall and the dining room," Helena instructed: "If there are any of you who do not value this proof of being well born, let those who do value this tradition have them." The rest, Helena may have believed, would be cast into hell fire—or at least into the increasingly casteless and thus, to her, flattened demographics of the modern world.

THREE

Born on Christmas Eve, 1904, in Richmond, Virginia, my mother Mary Clifford Caperton was the fifth of Helena Caperton's seven children. I discovered some of her papers in the blue box.

Helena's fifth pregnancy was in one way unique: while carrying Mary, she went abroad alone for several months in the fall of 1904, leaving her four older children with their grandmother Sallie (also at home were their father, their nurse, and two other servants), returning to Richmond just several weeks before Mary's birth. Though no letters from this period survive in the blue box, the timing of this journey was unusual. For a pregnant woman to travel at a period when the "interesting condition" often entailed a retreat from society, and to travel alone, was remarkable. Most likely Helena did not wander around Europe but visited her father's Lefroy relatives in Ulster or her aunts Minna and Mary in Sussex. Still, it was a display of independence at a time when most women would have stayed at home.

Perhaps her husband, Clifford, or her mother, Sallie, objected to Helena's escape, which left them to care for six-year-old Arthur, five-year-old Rose, three-year-old Helena, and two-year-old Sarah; perhaps they understood that the reprieve was essential for the heavily-burdened young mother and kept these objections to themselves.

Helena named her fifth child Mary, presumably in honor of her Aunt Mary Lefroy. She called her, at least briefly, Star of the Sea, a reference to the Mary prayed to by mariners as guiding light and sovereign of the ocean.

Mary Clifford Caperton, circa 1907   *Mary Clifford Caperton*

From the beginning Mary set herself apart from her sisters, displaying an unusual determination. She found her way to books at a young age and escaped into their stories for respite from her big, lively, contentious Richmond family.

While Helena mined their family life for comedy in her short stories and articles, Mary felt its harsh constraints in everything from missing the state fair because her mother couldn't afford to buy tickets for all her daughters to the difficulties of finding tuition for the private education Mary wanted.

She was encouraged by grandmother Sallie, who, according to Mary's oral history, "took the greatest interest in encouraging and fostering a love of reading. Her gentle but persistent correction of our grammar gave us an early start in right usage," which would become one of Mary's passions.

Mary remembered her grandmother explaining, "When you say 'She invited Sarah and I to dinner,' you may always test for error by dropping 'Sarah.' You would never say, 'She invited I to dinner.'" Sarah was Mary's older sister; after Mary came Harriette and Melinda.

Even more pointedly, Sallie suggested, "You love your mother, you do not love shad roe. You like shad roe."

According to Mary's oral history, her grandmother Sallie

> was a constant refuge, and had always a sympathetic, but firmly just answer to our problems and difficulties. She was often a last resort in differences that rose between us and Mother and Father. In a family of seven children, such opportunities for difficulties were frequent.

As when little Helena ran away from home, Sallie, called Artown by her grandchildren—a contraction of "Arthur's own"—was often the ultimate peacemaker. "She was a wonderfully equitable, cheerful, generous sort of person. We really loved her dearly. She was a great resort for all of us" as the babies continued to arrive.

Her father's influence seems to have been slight, although Mary would have noticed Clifford's fade from handsome young husband to unsuccessful traveling salesman. Mary did remember with horror her mother's rage at the end of every month when Clifford couldn't pay the household bills. These scenes were often resolved in bed and these parental rapprochements horrified her even more.

Mary, like her sisters, began her formal education at Miss Jenny Ellett's school on Laurel Street, eventually St. Catherine's School: "I remember Miss Lulie Blaire" [a long-lived teacher who had, in her youth, taught Mary's grandmother Sallie] "and the rest were awfully good teachers. Good at basics, reading and things."

Jenny Ellett was apparently a remarkable woman whose gleaming white tombstone in Richmond's Hollywood Cemetery stands out from the dark stones around it. Adorned with an engraving, in profile, of an elegant Miss Jenny wearing a large hat, the inscription reads,

> Foremost in learning and faith and aid
> Preeminent all tireless, never fond
> But resolute in progress and afraid
> Only of finding no more work beyond.

Her front-parlor girls' school would grow and prosper as it became St. Catherine's; still in operation, the school boasts as its contemporary axiom, "Empowering girls for a lifetime." Miss Ellett took a particular interest in Mary. Clearly, this Caperton daughter was full of potential, already more dedicated to learning than her sisters, and decidedly independent.

Mary, June Queen and Graduate, St. Catherine's School; photo from Richmond Times-Dispatch

Sophisticated teachers like Miss Ellett allowed certain girls, at least, to escape the low professional expectations typical for early twentieth-century women. Mary's exceptional ability might never have been discovered or developed if the Laurel Street school had not existed.

Mary always felt she was unlike her sisters, a difference symbolized by her plainness, or so she thought. This belief allowed her to focus on her intellectual life, rather than on clothes and beaux as her sisters did.

"They were all awfully pretty," Mary recalled. "I think I was considered the ugly one, sort of a blue stocking." But her avowed frumpiness is contradicted by her 1922 portrait as St. Catherine's May Queen, an honor bestowed on the senior who best represented the school's ideals. In a white dress, surrounded with baskets of white roses, Mary looks attractive, and certainly as blond and delicate as any of her sisters.

The six Caperton sisters competed for attention, which Helena did not discourage, believing the girls needed "hardening" in order to deal with the world. As teenagers they had to share one pair of silk stockings; they devised a system for passing them around. When Harriette (who according to her mother had "no sense of meum and tuum"—of mine and thine) wore them out of turn to the movies, her sisters protested to their mother. Helena telephoned the cinema and had the manager summon Harriette home over the public address system.

Harriette was Mary's only sister to escape Richmond for the purpose of finding work. "She had been a very talented young dancer," Mary remembered, "and so she left when I think she was about eighteen . . . to seek her fortune in New York."

Mary's eldest sister, Rose, did not pursue a career, but instead married at eighteen. Mary found her husband—the first of two—

> rather alarming. . . . He had a black moustache and he was very chic in his uniform, satin brown belt and polished boots. And his stick . . . I can't remember what they called the stick, it was perfectly useless except to add to the panache of the uniform. Anyhow I thought it a very romantic affair. It turned out to be a miserable marriage.

Mary was much closer to her sister Sarah: "She was very small, much shorter than the rest of us and a most dynamic and positive sort of person."

Her other sisters seemed to have blurred together in Mary's memory.

Mary barely mentioned her departure from home in 1922, when she was eighteen, saying only, "I went and lived with Louise Burleigh for a while.... Several years, two years, I think." She didn't explain what precipitated her decision to leave home and move in with her friend Louise. It's clear, however, that she was leaving behind the turbulence and economic uncertainty of her parents' household forever.

She complained, in that same oral history, that Helena had forced her to drop out of school before graduating to concentrate on playing the violin, thus making her miss vital preparation for college. Mary and her mother must have quarreled fiercely and perhaps the move came as the result of this impasse.

Whatever its causes, Mary's choice of housemate said much about her intellectual aspirations. In the early 1920s, Louise Burleigh was an accomplished professional woman, unlike Helena, Sallie, or their Richmond friends, and she became a profound influence on young Mary Caperton.

Born in 1889 in New Hampshire, and thus fifteen years older than Mary, Louise had entered Radcliffe College in 1908 and became a charter member of a renowned course in theatre offered at Harvard by Dr. George Pierce Baker: Workshop 47. Louise had also been deeply involved in the Idler Club, Radcliffe's drama society, writing in 1911, "It binds the college together in a social sense. It does for Radcliffe what dormitory life, sororities, and athletics do for Smith, Vassar, and Wellesley."

Louise's love of theatre had begun when, at seven years old, she was taken by her father to see *Twelfth Night* and became so excited that he forbad her to see any other plays for the next seven years, an astonishing tribute to the liveliness of her personality and the constraints imposed on her.

After college she began a career as actor, playwright, and organizer of community theatres. That work, detailed in her book, *The Community Theatre in Theory and Practice*, published in 1917 by Little, Brown and Company, gradually replaced her acting, although not until a number of years after she made her 1912 professional debut in Boston, playing the title role in a play called *Little Boy of the World*. Tiny, with close-cropped hair and an infectious chuckle, Louise kept her little-boy look for the rest of her life.

When Mary met her, Louise had been brought to Richmond to run the Little Theatre League after its founder was killed in World War I. Louise had been noticed nationally for her 1916 production, at New York's Portmanteau Theatre, of the Restoration comedy *Gammer Gurton's Needle*. This bawdy sixteenth-century farce remained her best-known production.

In Richmond, Louise tried to produce a play based on James Branch Cabell's *Jurgen, A Comedy of Justice* (1919), a novel that had scandalized Richmond society and thus made fundraising for the play impossible. This setback did nothing to discourage Louise, who found in theatre "the expression of joy through art." She aimed to fit theatre to the "yoke of democracy," protesting that, "instead of social theatres, we have had society theatres." She admired the Neighborhood Playhouse in New York, believing it gave "exquisite expression to the beauty sleeping in the mind of the long silenced Jewish people." When she moved to Richmond, she firmly believed that the participation of the audience—the more diverse audience she hoped to attract—was essential to the health of the theatre.

Settling in Richmond at 106 North Plum Street, Louise and her long-time assistant, Lydia Harrison, turned their tiny house into a haven for women trying to escape the limitations of Richmond life. For twelve years, Louise took her productions to remote hamlets in Virginia and West Virginia where she cast her plays with local people.

After Mary joined her household, Louise encouraged her to seek a scholarship to Radcliffe while providing her with a home, and an ambience, distinctly different from West Avenue. North Plum Street was unconventional, even racy—a place where Mary met interesting women her mother and grandmother didn't know. There, she was encouraged to act, and was, during her stay, cast as the ribald character of Dame Chat in Louise's Richmond production of *Gammer Gurton's Needle*.

In her oral history, Mary went to some lengths to explain that, by 1922, Louise was already in love with her future husband, John Powell. Powell was a well-known Virginia composer, pianist, and musicologist, and even before their engagement Louise spent countless hours with him, long into the night. When friends and acquaintances asked Mary what was going on in the house on North Plum Street, she replied that Louise and John were working on musical compositions; she could say so with authority because, she said, she was with the couple every minute.

Despite her kind and crucial encouragement of Mary's intellectual life, Louise Burleigh's own trajectory was already beginning its decline. In 1921, in Richmond, Louise and John Powell had begun working together on *Beatrice: A Tragedy in One Act*, a pedantic and racist morality play that purported to explore the fate of a "tragic mullata." Throughout his life, and beyond this play, Powell was obsessed with eugenics; he promoted the Racial Integrity Act, calling for registration "showing the racial composition" of Virginians in order to forbid "miscegenation." The act was signed into law in 1924 and remained on the books in Virginia until superseded by a federal law in 1962, the year of Powell's death.

In 1928, several weeks before Mary's graduation from Radcliffe, Louise Burleigh married John Powell and abandoned her own work in theatre, explaining, "Two careers in a family like ours are bound to clash." He seems a curious choice for this formerly lively, independent, progressive woman. His artistic reputation, as a collector of folk music and a successful composer, soon outshone hers. But he was first and foremost a rigid authoritarian whose politics clashed, at least initially, with Louise's beliefs. Friends remembered that his racist outbursts sometimes caused her to argue vehemently, stamping her foot. At times she was so angry that she had to leave the room, but she ultimately came to endorse Powell's agenda.

Sadly, John Powell's fascination with eugenics affected Mary deeply, providing her with the illusion of a scientific basis to excuse the racist attitudes she had imbibed since birth. With tacit endorsement from society through means as widely varied as Virginia's miscegenation laws and the Holocaust, the eugenics myth has distorted judgment and destroyed lives. Mary's own belief, partly concealed, in this insidious myth influenced her attitude throughout far too much of her life, limiting her ability to navigate the changing society around her and, later, to help her children do the same.

Yet her escape to Louise's house also allowed her to finish her thwarted high school education and pursue the Radcliffe degree that would ultimately enable her to leave her family, and Louise Burleigh's Richmond, behind.

Mary did indeed graduate from St. Catherine's, though not until 1923. A portrait taken around that time shows an intense, even somber young woman, her sharp gaze accentuated by dark eyebrows, her shapely mouth set in a half smile. If the photograph is correctly dated, she graduated at nineteen. The school's intellectual rigor and insistence on Richmond's socially approved values would influence her for the rest of her life.

As Mary began her freshman year at Radcliffe in the fall of 1924— escorted there by Louise—her life for the first time foreshadows mine; I entered the freshman class at Radcliffe thirty years later, in 1954.

Settling in her grim little room at Bertram Hall, Mary would have looked out over a broad lawn barricaded with the high-shouldered buildings of the other Radcliffe dormitories. Outside, girls sat on the grass, alone or in clusters, soaking up the early autumn sun.

How lonely Mary felt, as though she had arrived "from Katmandu," she remembered, entering the dorm's living room where bridge games were already in progress, or the dining room where knots of boarding school friends chatted together. The other girls would have noticed, first, Mary's Virginia accent (my less-refined Kentucky accent provoked questions about wearing shoes), then her diminutive size, blond bob, and marked hauteur.

As she imagined, they might actually have assumed she was some kind of foreigner or alien—they were nearly all from New England—but her sense of superiority as the daughter of one of Virginia's first families protected her from feeling any slights too keenly.

A scholarship girl, she joined what was then a significant minority. Unlike the more fashionable women's colleges of the 1920s, Radcliffe gave scholarships to a full twenty-five percent of its students. Referred to as "The Annex," just as it was in my day, the college had dormitories, a gym, and a library but no faculty of its own. Since its chartering in 1894, the college granted degrees signed by both Harvard and Radcliffe, and, often against opposition, sent its girls to classes at Harvard. All Mary's professors were men, as mine would be.

In 1920, women already comprised forty-seven percent of the United States' collegiate student body, yet Mary's Radcliffe experience was still marked by institutional and academic sexism.

After settling into her room, Mary walked through quiet residential streets to Harvard Yard to enroll in the required freshman courses. She attended classes on the Harvard campus, sitting with a small group of girls in the big lecture halls, often presided over by professors of some renown.

The somber atmosphere did not encourage questions; the girls were nearly always silent as they took their meticulous notes. They wore their own version of a uniform: pleated wool skirts, low-heeled leather shoes with stockings, blouses with dainty collars, cardigans, and, as the weather cooled, heavy woolen coats. They generally obeyed the college's request that they wear hats and gloves. Some knitted; legend had it that, at Smith, a lecturing professor became so irritated by the sound of clacking needles that he told the girls that knitting was a substitute for masturbation.

As winter came on, the classroom radiators clanged, and rain brought the stench of soaked wool and rubber overshoes. By midwinter, the big overhead lights were on all day, as they were in Widener Library where Radcliffe girls were not allowed to study. Instead, these female students were assigned to a room with chintz-covered furniture in the basement of Memorial Hall. In later years, I retreated there, too.

Although Mary claimed later that she was poorly prepared, she made A's in all her freshman classes. Her essays were carefully researched and reasoned, neatly typed (without corrections), and each was headed, "M. Caperton, Bertram Hall, Cambridge, Mass."

In the blue box, I found numerous essays from her early days at Radcliffe, essays which she kept for the rest of her life. One, dated May 1925—her sophomore year—is titled, "Not From the Missouri Flats," apparently in reference to its subject, an Appalachian folk song that had evolved from an older ballad of the British Isles. Mary uses this song and its precursor to advance an idea that became central to her budding philosophy: "dumb repression" is a more effective means of communication than "the hysterical exclamatory manner." She did not envision a middle path.

To support this thesis, she writes that the briefer, simpler Appalachian folk verse has a "greater depth of tragedy" and "seems greater and somehow more mature" than the earlier, more expansive

English ballad on which the verse is based. After giving Mary's paper an A, her professor comments vaguely, "Very interesting, but perhaps there is something to be said on the other side." Though there is indeed, Mary apparently did not go looking for it: the more complex language that reveals greater emotional depths. A longer, more thoughtful essay, titled "A Rationalization of Guido's Case," examines Robert Browning's four-volume work, *The Ring and the Book.*

After summarizing the plot, Mary suggests, "Does not a fifty-year-old man look rather a fool for marrying a girl of fifteen?"

In the margin, her professor replies, "Well, rather, nowadays! Though, to be sure, for various state and economic reasons, he would have looked less a fool in Guido's day."

Mary believes that Guido, tried for his wife's murder in Rome in 1698, is not presented "impartially" in the poem because of Browning's "admitted bias for Pompilia" [Guido's wife], a bias Mary doesn't share. "The romantic imagination is too paramount," and so Guido's chances of fair treatment are "slim." She believes he is suffering from "an acute inferiority complex" because he comes from "a lineage that lack the flag yet lifts the pole"—like her Virginia family, "full of the corroding bitterness of a land poor aristocracy." Her description of Guido's predicament appears to be an unacknowledged tribute to her own henpecked and "land poor" father.

She explains that Guido, "old enough to want respite from emotional scenes, seemingly viciously baulked by circumstance," would be intensely irritated by Pompilia, "this model of spotless perfection which beat its wings frantically against the bars of his subtly aroused brutality, or rushed about making public the most intimate affairs of his personal life.... Is it surprising that he killed her?" Surely any sympathy she had for her father would not have extended to excusing him if he took Guido's path and murdered her mother, but it may have come close.

This essay points to Mary's growing propensity to understand and excuse men, often blaming their transgressions on women who had indulged in, as she wrote earlier, "the hysterical exclamatory manner" and who must take responsibility for men's "subtly aroused brutality." If a girl's manner could inspire an attack, she was not only, inevitably, a victim, she was also to blame.

And yet—and yet—in some deeply recessed corner of her personality, which she would never explore, Mary may have found comfort in taking responsibility for others' cruelty: to be the cause of one's own suffering can be less terrifying than to suffer inexplicable iniquities.

This essay and the ones that follow raise the question of whether the ideas and opinions of Mary's Richmond childhood were altered by her experiences at Harvard. The professors who influenced her most, such as Irving Babbitt, reinforced her childhood prejudices; the glowing comments and high grades she received, like the glowing reviews for Helena's ventures into the grotesque, made it less likely that she would question her ideas. Her paper on Browning's Guido evoked a comment that would be repeated: "Yes, this is the real thing! Your manner is excellent talk, and your matter is clear-sighted to a degree that one does not look for in persons under forty!"

Praising an essay as "excellent talk" would be surprising today, but in academic circles in the 1920s, brilliant conversation, especially for women, was the hallmark of a fine mind and an end in itself. Academic papers might molder unread, but a woman, especially an attractive woman, who could entrance with her voice and her use of words (an upper-class Virginia accent helped) would always win approbation.

Mary's unnamed professor, as he graded her "Rationalization," was of the same mind. He goes on rapturously,

> Do you know of anyone else to whom the same idea has occurred? I confess I don't. . . . I want to drain the last drop of excitement

from this report, and to know the idea as well as the working out was your own would finish me!

Perhaps realizing that his excitement might seem excessive, he adds, "To be sure, Professor Babbitt in his pronouncements on the subject gives a hint of what you do, but barely a hint."

Mary took at least one course with Professor Babbitt during her Radcliffe career, when he was at the height of his influence as a proponent of the New Humanism; at Harvard, he was a constant critic of Romanticism in all its forms, as Mary grew to be.

Her embrace of Babbitt's New Humanism did not diminish her sense of humor; Mary's dry wit glitters in all her papers. During her first two years in college, they never earned less than a B plus, and her teachers' comments were unusually flattering.

Although all Mary's papers received top grades, they do not exhibit much original thinking; meticulously written, thick with footnotes and quotations, they are rather self-consciously scholarly. She seems to have been taught at Harvard not how to think but what to think. Helena would have been proud of her grades but perplexed by her constant citations, and possibly bored.

Mary's college life was not all studying. The 1920s were careening and crashing around her: Prohibition made drinking bootleg alcohol seem like a rebellion against conventionality. Many college students patronized speakeasies and carried hip flasks. At Radcliffe, Mary drank, kept her hair bobbed, shortened her skirts, and began to smoke.

Radcliffe might disapprove, but nothing could prevent the students' carousing, although "parietal hours"—the infamous "in loco parentis" exercised by dormitory "mothers" until the early 1960s—forced the Radcliffe girls back to their beds before midnight.

Even as more social possibilities unfolded, Mary devoted herself to her studies, deciding to major in Classical Studies with a minor in Elizabethan Drama. Her professors and the writers she studied were all men. Mary herself wasn't quite ready to believe the opposite sex could compare.

She was, however, enthusiastic about the only modern novel about which she wrote an essay: Henry James's *What Maisie Knew*. This essay, which earned her another A, puts forward the disastrous effects of Maisie's parents' divorce and subsequent misbehavior:

> She [Maisie] knew. She always did know, by an education which had taught her to realize in difficult situations in what direction the wind was blowing, how to meet her parents' tantrums with apparent solidity, and which finally evolved in her a set of sort of social antennae, which helped her little anxious mind to her greatest desire: to be a peacemaker.

The unusual awkwardness and surprising empathy of Mary's lengthy sentence is telling. Mary writes as the fifth child in a chaotic Richmond household, the daughter who always "knew" and tried to broker peace between her wrangling parents, even when it came at the price of the distasteful evidence of their physical encounters.

She describes the reader's feeling toward Maisie's stepfather: "We can't help liking Sir Claude very much as a man of more than human charm, in his weakness, his helplessness in a situation which certainly he had never bargained for"—like her own father, Clifford Caperton, who she must have thought could not have "bargained for" the responsibilities that fell on him with marriage and seven children.

Mary especially admires Sir Claude's elevation of his stepdaughter into "a relation of pure equality" which seems to depend on changing her gender; on their intimate jaunts together, he calls Maisie "my old man."

"It is a great novel," she concludes, "one of desperate realism."

•

By her junior year, her reading list was impressive; she was comfortable with German as well as classical Greek. In the spring semester, she writes enthusiastically about Sappho, praising the writer for creating "the illusion of radiance in her poetry."

Here Mary insisted that, when reading Sappho, "The reader is forced, in his effort to create a visual image, to settle on an exact color implied by a desperate effort of the imagination." In her example, the Greek term for hyacinth blue "does not take into account the hyacinth's many shades of blue from a deep almost purple to a blue almost white"—a description of impressions she may have picked up in a Richmond garden.

But why is this exercise of the imagination "desperate"? Throughout her life Mary often referred to imagination as a forceful, even frightening effort, revealing the conflict she always felt between Helena's rigid Richmond pieties and the less socially acceptable version of reality the imagination, as in theatre or poetry, might create. She goes on:

> I shudder at using the word creative, it has been so ruined, but it does seem to me that to enjoy Sappho properly requires an exertion of the imagination—not only the "willing suspension of disbelief which constitutes poetic faith" but even an active use of the imagination, as Coleridge elsewhere said, as a unifying power.

By contrast, Pindar earns her esteem more readily because of his "appreciation of wealth and youth, beauty and physical prowess, [which] makes more effective, throws into relief, his piety and god-fearing humility."

The language of the Episcopal Church—those Sunday mornings

around the corner at St. James—continued to furnish Mary with a context for her readings in classical Greek literature.

In an examination bluebook, Mary illuminates a passage in Homer she has been asked to translate:

> If "aty" may be translated "sin," the whole passage recalls Peter V.8: "Be sober, be vigilant, because your adversary, the devil, as the roaring lion, walks about, seeking whom he may devour."
>
> There is more opulent imagery here, but Homer is cleverer. Surely Aty, swift of foot and might, going about his enticing ways is a more subtle enemy than a roaring lion seeking whom he may devour—an apparition whom almost anyone with discernment would naturally avoid.

Of all the essays from the blue box, Mary saves her harshest condemnation for Clytemnestra. She fulminates, "It is this shameless and arrogant assumption of virtue that dampens our sympathy for Clytemnestra. . . . Her boldness, which is enough to make the elders blush to the roots, must have completely cowed these old men." When confronting Clytemnestra's story, Mary could not, perhaps, see beyond Helena's rages at her cowed husband. The termagant of the Richmond parlor was loose again.

Mary equally deplored "the wild and barbaric elements of the early worship of Demeter and the dread goddess Persephone." Why does Demeter's ravished daughter, who ate the pomegranate seeds and so was condemned to spend part of each year in Hades, seem to Mary to merit the adjective "dread"? She knew her goddesses; this was not an ignorant mistake. Was it Persephone's power to cause her mother anguish? Or was it Mary's belief in the power of female purity to arouse male violence—the maiden too maidenish to survive in her field of flowers?

It remains a mystery, but a telling one. For Mary, who witnessed her mother's rages, believed her father a victim, and felt lost in a tangle of sisters, the Demeter-Persephone story may have hinted at a terrible revenge: rob the mother of her beloved daughter and plunge the world into winter. Persephone, to such an angry daughter, would certainly deserve to be called "dread."

George Barry Bingham

In the spring of 1927, Mary met the handsome blond heir to a Kentucky fortune, Barry Bingham, who was studying at Harvard. At the end of her long life, Mary described their romance as "so innocent, really, so delightful." In what may be his first letter to Mary, now archived in the Filson Historical Society, Barry wrote from a hotel in Brewster, Massachusetts, in May:

> As usual with me since my life has taken its sudden change.and great bound upward, in other words since I've been in love with you, I want to tell you everything that has happened to me.

He and Warren Buckler, a college classmate who reappeared in many letters and remained a lifelong friend, drove from Cambridge "in a sickening rain and fog." They planned to spend the weekend studying. Barry started with "a drab chapter" from *Madame Bovary*, describing his studious position: "Sitting up in bed with both legs doubled up under me, actually enjoying the luxury of a little reading lamp with a yellow chintz shade."

Next day, walking on the beach in "the loveliest cloudless blue morning," then eating "a great dish of steamed clams, throwing melted butter all over the table" while Warren devoured five dinner rolls, later soaking up the sun—"The wind rippled over our poor old hides in the most delicious way"—and finally playing the *Blue Danube* on the hotel parlor phonograph, the two young men must have created a joyous scenario.

To top it off, "In came the hostess with a letter. Your letter! You're such a completely adorable person to have written me so soon, and such a thrilling and provocative letter!" which, unfortunately, he didn't save.

What did the Richmond girl offer that would be "thrilling" and "provocative"? Both, at this point in their lives, were probably virgins; the mandates of their upbringing prohibited premarital sex, or at least mention thereof.

Yet the times were changing; the Jazz Age offered new possibilities of liberty and self-expression, and although Mary was not herself a flapper, she was part of the liberated world of the 1920s, and she was looking for a way to intrigue a young man born into endless opportunity.

Perhaps by hinting at thrills she never actually provided, she kept his interest alive without challenging him with the demands of intimacy. In any case, the result was an elaborate pas de deux danced to music only they could hear.

"Oh my sweet," Barry wrote, "your letter makes me see you so clearly. I think I know how you looked when you wrote every phrase" from her dormitory room.

But, in contrast to this enthusiasm, he was "startled" to learn that Mary planned to come to Brewster, chaperoned by engaged friends. It seemed a sudden, even a surprising move; after all, she wasn't invited.

Over the course of the letter, he talked himself into it: "Now that I think it over, I don't see why it's not a perfectly good idea. You absolutely must come. I've built all my plans around seeing you on Sunday."

Yet his initial hesitation lingered, as when he warned, "There's absolutely nothing to do here but picnic and swim," adding that the train schedule would only allow them a few hours together.

After more equivocation about trains, he offered another, final encouragement:

> My darling Mary, it's become an active physical privation for me to be separated from you. I'm glad our love is really so ecstatically happy when we're together, as it makes it worthwhile to go through a good deal of privation.

He closed with a line from Shakespeare's *All's Well That Ends Well*: "This thorn/doth to our rose of youth rightly belong."

Barry's next letter, written a few weeks later, informed Mary that he was going away again, this time to an inn in Pomfret, Connecticut. He needed "nine hours of work a day that I can't accomplish in Cambridge. I'd so much rather be near you when I study . . . but Massachusetts Hall is chaos since vacation began."

Describing Pomfret in loving detail, confident of Mary's interest in his life's minutiae, Barry noted one store that sold post cards, mainly, for some strange reason, views of Rotterdam, Holland, and some fly-blown bars of chocolate.

I thought at first that I had left my comb in Cambridge, and I verily believe if I had I would have been compelled to walk to Putnam for another or gone back to college looking like a Gorgon.

Five-course meals and the conversation of "old ladies who play whist at night and talk about New York, inspired by a box of Page and Shaw candy" delighted him almost as much as his room, "with windows on two sides and low hills rolling away for a long way to the South." On trips such as these he began a lifelong love affair with New England.

Happy in his weekend schedule, "I can do nine hours of work and walk at least two hours a day," he reassured her, adding, "I love you, my dearest, and I'd give anything in the world to see you walking up the road"—but he didn't ask her to visit and this time, she didn't appear.

Barry included two of his own poems in this letter, with apologies. One, titled "Paradise," ends with an odd allusion to other, or perhaps ex-, lovers:

Adam sometimes turned from Eve's embrace
To dream of earlier nights, and Lilith's eyes. . . .
Some say that Eden was a lonely place.

In June 1927, a few months after they met and just after their junior year ended, Barry left Cambridge to visit his Aunt Sadie Grinnan in Asheville, North Carolina. Sadie had taken the place of his mother after her early death. Along with other relatives involved in the running of the now-closed Bingham Military School, she lived in what had been the headmaster's house, perched on a hillside over the French Broad River.

As she recalled later, before Barry left, Mary asked him if he would still love her in the fall. He replied with airy nonchalance that he couldn't be sure.

On Bingham Military School letterhead—adorned with its motto, "Mens Sana in Corpus Sano," under an eagle—he wrote to Mary, "You're a darling to write me soon, as you promised, and particularly after such a strenuous evening in the rarefied Liberal Club atmosphere."

Charmingly self-deprecating (with just a hint of condescension), he indulged briefly in some scholarly banter, writing:

> Darling child, do you wish I could talk to you about the relation of critical humanism and Progress (with a Philistine interpretation?). I'm a washout conversationally when I'm with you, I'm afraid, because all I want to say is, "I love you," and that's not news even to you. Do you think I'm a terrible nitwit?

In Asheville, he delighted in a "pastoral vacation," describing for her "a bank of periwinkles that are just the color your eyes were last Sunday on the way to Wellesley."

Mary was not enjoying a pastoral vacation; she had stayed in New England, working in a tea shop and taking care of her friend Mildred Penn's children. By 1927 her scholarship had proved inadequate, and she was barely getting by on part-time work and Mildred's bounty.

Barry writes that, since he arrived in Asheville, he's spent "the whole time telling various relatives all about what I've been doing for the last year"—without, as it turned out, mentioning Mary. Four years later, when they finally became engaged, his Aunt Sadie needed to ask if Mary was an Episcopalian and a Democrat—satisfyingly, she was— having apparently never heard anything about her.

Barry did, however, tell Mary about his own family, writing to her
that Colonel Bingham, Barry's grandfather and the last headmaster of
the school, was "very weak and really as old as the hills. He doesn't want
any Scott right now" and so his grandson was reading him newspaper
accounts of events in China. (This Colonel Bingham is the terrifying
old curmudgeon whom Thomas Wolfe gleefully caricatured in *Look
Homeward, Angel* as the headmaster rounding up errant schoolboys in
Asheville on Saturday nights.)

Barry was relieved that the old man hadn't asked to hear

> some of the books of the Old Testament . . . I'm sure I'd
> mispronounce the kings of Judah and the children they begat
> and I'd get hell for my ignorance. It's remarkable how ignorant a
> junior at Harvard can be.

Again, he lamented his inarticulateness: "My 'erotic vocabulary' is
rotten. You were so perfectly beautiful Thursday night on the steps" of
her dormitory "and later when I kissed you goodbye, but I couldn't tell
you. All I could do was kiss you." His ineloquent eloquence served him
well, as he must have known.

"When I get back to you again, do you think things will be
different?" he asked, echoing Mary's earlier question. "Personally I
don't see how it's possible for you to go on caring for me when I'm
away. . . . You haven't had a chance to make a habit of caring for me."
Nor had he.

"Damn you," the letter ends, "You asked me not to forget you, but
it's so useless, because I can't." He added, in a poignant aside, "I never
knew love was so complicated and so hard to express."

With her sharp wit, Mary might have been tempted to eviscerate
Barry's sentimentality, but doubtless his effusions meant too much to
her to examine them critically. Lacking her letters, few of which Barry

saved, it's impossible to know. She kept his, some catalogued at the Filson Historical Society, others preserved more privately in the blue box, for the rest of her life.

Yet such overheated language, such passion expressed so early in a relationship confined by propriety to kisses, and such long absences— the summer of 1927 set a pattern for their frequent separations—with no plans for a shared future must have given her pause; engagements after a few months of courtship were the rule in her world. But whatever her misgivings, she never seriously considered another man.

Certainly Barry's money, inherited from a stepmother he disliked, added to his charm. By the time she came to Radcliffe, Mary had already seen too much of the constraints of genteel poverty; she had struggled just to pay for her education. She knew that the few women in academia, spinsters all, earned hardly more than a bare subsistence and lived in what was to her a social netherworld. This future never appealed to her.

Barry was gilded by his delightful humor and his smooth blond looks; in some photographs, he resembles F. Scott Fitzgerald—another Midwesterner bound for glory—whose writing he admired. And, for Mary, there was the attendant fascination of his lasting unavailability; while he was writing Mary, he was also seeing other women, most frequently two red-haired twins in Boston.

Beyond his fortune, there was the draw of his background. Although Mary never met the old Colonel, she had certainly heard of Bingham's *English Grammar*, written by an earlier Bingham Military School headmaster, William Bingham, and used for decades in schools all over the South.

Bingham's *English Grammar* was a rulebook after her own heart. In his preface to the 1867 edition, William Bingham wrote of himself in the orthodox third person: "In constructing definitions and rules, he has studied brevity and perspicuity, preferring plain English to words of foreign origin; and as far as possible the rules and definitions are identical with those in the Latin Grammar."

A thorough knowledge of linguistic "roots" might not have attracted many pretty Southern girls, but for Mary, "roots" represented a fundamental principal, not only in language but also in values.

A reverence for this fundamental principle that privileges heritage over all else runs throughout William's grammatical instruction; one of his "Parsing Exercises" quotes Addison's *On Ancestry*: "Naturally speaking, a man bids fairer for greatness of soul who is the descendant of worthy ancestors and has good blood in his veins than one who is come of an ignoble and obscure parentage." Like Barry's Bingham ancestor, Helena's daughter was well versed in society's elevation of Addison's "good blood."

Barry's lovely letters—written in his flowing cursive without blot or correction, and saved for so long in that hidden blue box—attest to what Mary found most precious in his background: tradition, heritage, education. And, above all, gorgeous language.

Barry wrote to Mary often during that first summer: from Melcombe, "The Big House," his father's house outside Louisville, Kentucky; from Scotland, where his father rented a castle for grouse-hunting; from his father's yacht; and finally from London, where Robert Bingham would be installed as American ambassador in 1933. His letters describe, deliriously, the pleasures of being young, handsome, rich, and unencumbered.

But he continued to draw attention to various impediments to his full expression, as in an earlier letter from Cambridge in which he apologized about a telephone call: "There sat Warren right by my side, listening to the whole conversation, so I had to restrain myself." Impossible to ask the attentive eavesdropper to remove himself.

He wrote further as if there was an impediment even in her presence: "I always feel so much the sensation of the pursuit of Daphne when I'm with you, I'm always so sure that you are too beautiful for me to hold in my arms for more than a moment." He seemed to be trying to convince himself that she was not pursuing him.

Her next letter was so potent that "It made me practically unable to get up the stairs." Even thus paralyzed, he joyously anticipated a reunion at "Harriet's House at Wayland and the Thunderbolt at Revere."

A rollercoaster known as The Thunderbolt figured in one of Barry's short stories, "White Carnation," published in Harvard's literary magazine, *The Advocate*, in 1925—two years before he and Mary met. The elegantly written tale is told from the point of view of a poor New York shop girl named Molly.

After a chance meeting, handsome John, a college student, takes Molly to Coney Island, where she begins to feel "a sharp desire to kiss this odd, detached boy" who looks "clean, his clear skin and white teeth and the funny smell about him of shaving soap and good cigarettes. She had never seen any boy take such genuine pleasure in doing ridiculous things." After enjoying the rides, Molly is ready "to give herself to John if he desired her," but at her door he only "bent and kissed her calmly, tenderly, as one would kiss a child," leaving her with the "wizened" white carnation she'd won in a booth. She walks Fifth Avenue for months, hoping to see him again, but when she does, he's with a date. "She saw him touch the girl's arm with an intimate caressing gesture that was somehow not just kind or friendly." Back in her dismal flat, Molly finally shreds the white carnation.

The story seems to reflect Barry's belief in, or fear of, his own ability to fascinate, as well as his potential for doing harm.

Almost an illustration for the story, a snapshot of Mary, Barry, and Warren walking down a Richmond street shows Mary sporting a lavish corsage; she did not need to shred her flowers. She and Barry were enjoying what he later described as a "musical comedy romance," with lots of drinking and dancing—and kissing.

Barry knew and loved Noël Coward's plays. The tone of the relationship he established, which was perhaps not exactly the relationship Mary wanted, was tinged with Coward's insouciance. No matter how passionate his letters, they were always light, fantastical, verging on the ironic. Mary may have wondered whether to take them seriously.

One of the vulnerabilities of letter-writing is that the writer must embrace the shaky belief that words themselves—the right words—have an inherent integrity and exist, somehow, in their own right, independent of the whims of the speaker—or the reader. Elegant, well-turned language not only expresses, it implies the existence of strong emotion, as in poetry, idealistic political speeches, and love letters. Barry's letters are lavish, and yet they seem oddly insubstantial, like declarations of love in a Coward comedy.

Later in that summer of 1927, Barry wrote Mary from Kentucky to say that he had been rushing around "like a squirrel in a cage, definitely getting nowhere. . . . There's a party every night," and only once in two weeks had he gone to bed before dawn.

He described sleeping in the Big House on "a porch up in the trees in what has always been the children's part of the house"—the big sleeping porch with its four single beds and huge screened windows.

He lingered on a description of his leisurely days:

It is lovely to go to bed just before sunrise, with a pink sky, wakening birds, and all the embellishments of a sentimental ballad. . . . I slip under a cool sheet, place two pillows neatly beneath my head, and think about you till I fall asleep. . . . I wake up sometime during the morning with the sun moving solemnly over my bed, and think of you in different ways, and then with a

great effort rush out of bed and down the hill, and after a quick
shedding of pajamas, into the cool green water of the pool.

The pool at the Big House was a huge concrete tank, painted a flaking
blue, filled by hose, and home to frogs, tadpoles, and spiders.

Barry continued, "I can't imagine myself ever breaking away from
my present habits, of riding in the morning, playing tennis in the
afternoon, and carousing in the evening. I want to say all kinds of
ridiculous things that can't be said in a letter."

After this intimate impulse, he turned to a description of Mary's
sister Helena's broken engagement to a "famous four-flusher"—a
derogatory term derived from poker for a cheat—from Louisville who,
as Barry had learned, possessed far less money than he had led Helena
to believe. The man's family intervened in the couple's plans because,
Barry explained, although they knew that Helena comes from "the
best family in Richmond, she has the reputation of being a little broad-
minded." In other words, the family decided, because of rumors they'd
heard, that it was unlikely that Helena was a virgin. Barry added that
his informant had no idea he knew Helena's sister.

The family's intervention didn't stop the four-flusher from buying
"an impressive car, hiring a chauffeur, and taking your mother and
Helena on a tour of the eastern resorts." The older Helena must have
enjoyed it thoroughly.

In a later letter, Barry apologized for passing on this gossip.
He explained that Helena's suitor was "only a child in his actions,"
although already married and divorced, with two daughters. His family
considered him "an attractive but irresponsible member who has to be
taken care of by his more balanced relatives." In the end, the couple
renewed their engagement; Helena married this man and endured
years of alcoholic tumult.

More Louisville gossip followed. Peggy and Jim, the couple who chaperoned Barry and Mary back in the spring, were presumably engaged, but Barry reported that Peggy was no longer coming to Louisville because, as Jim told him, "she couldn't make the grade"— the first hint of the power of Barry's hometown's expectations.

Then Barry described reading some Greek lyrics in the garden, where he sat

> under a pergola, with the sunlight floating down in golden discs through the vines. The garden smelt warm and sweet with a mingling of odors, and the bees lumbered about among the flowers, and everything was still and expectant.

A trip on his father's yacht ensued in July. They sailed to Nantucket:

> I like it better than any place I've ever seen. Have you been there? I've made up my mind that I must live here for one whole year and see every season on this wild, windy landscape. It is bleak in a way.

Forty years later he would fly to Nantucket to retrieve the body of his eldest son, killed at thirty-five there in a driving accident.

In the summer of 1927, though, the island reminded him that "I always wanted someone to share emotion with me from the earliest things I can remember, and quite naturally, all my desire for companionship has centered on you."

Then, about to leave for Europe, he reassured Mary about his return, writing that "Father is getting me [return] space on the *Majestic*, sailing to New York on August 24, which delights my soul. I wish to hell I was with you on Putney Hill"—Mildred and Ramon Penn's place, where Mary was ensconced during her working summers, in Hopkinton, New Hampshire.

By the writing of his next letter, Barry had rushed off to meet his sister Henrietta at the Ritz in New York; in less than an hour, their boat would embark for Europe. He apologized for his farewell phone call to Mary as "entirely inadequate."

Acknowledging their inability to find time together over the course of the summer, he wrote, "We have spent most of our time since we loved each other in the center of a maelstrom of humanity," and then suggested, "we detach ourselves a little in the fall. . . . I love kissing you behind screens and doors, but I'm afraid my happiness makes other people irritable." The suggestion could not have pleased Mary who might have found his excuse peculiar. Who was made irritable? And why? His reference to his beloved sister Henrietta may have provided a clue.

Something had happened that spring that Mary regretted, which may explain his sudden need for detachment, although Barry also declared, "It was the sweetest experience of my life to hold you in my arms at Peggy's, though I felt desperately helpless and ineffectual."

Whatever happened at Peggy's, or didn't, he wrote, "At least once we have meant a definite individual part of each other's lives"—a curious circumlocution.

By this time, Mary knew she needed a decisive act to capture this elusive quarry. Giving herself—in the parlance of the time—to him was an option, one that would have brought the sexual liberation of the 1920s crashing headlong into the proscriptions of her childhood. Mary's mother, Helena, had long viewed premarital sex as a "millstone" dragging any young woman down to the depths; no suitable man, she believed, would marry a young woman who had so lowered herself in his eyes.

If Mary regretted whatever happened at Peggy's, surely it was because it didn't prompt the declaration she wanted. If she was upset, it was because she had violated her standards, in whatever mysterious way, to no purpose. If Barry's admission of being "helpless" and "ineffectual" was an allusion to impotence, the occasion may have been miserably uncomfortable for both of them. In any event, the experiment was, if not repeated, at least never referred to again in these letters.

Despite his urge toward distance, Barry still hoped to receive a letter from Mary at the Boston pier, even though "it's a little difficult to explain the meaning of the sudden secret smiles, chuckles, and even loud laughs" her letters always evoked, especially since his relatives didn't know who was writing to him.

Next, a letter from Guthrie Castle in Scotland, where Barry was grouse hunting with his father, described raising the spirits every night by table-tipping with Henrietta and her friends at their impromptu séances.

Guthrie Castle near Dundee in Angus, Scotland, became a regular stopping-off place in Barry's family peregrinations. Although parts of the building date to the fifteenth century, most of it was built in the nineteenth. The castle particularly suited Barry and Henrietta because it was said to be haunted; at one of their table-tipping sessions, Barry claimed, the table escaped and flew around the room.

While in Scotland, he wrote that he had been

> overcome by the hopelessness of expressing what I feel to you from so far away, and oppressed by a great loneliness that has made me rush away in search of something diverting to allay the pain. . . . My love for you seems avid of nearness, and I'm more or less like a shade wandering and gibbering in Limbo when I am removed far from you.

But he could always find diversions.

At the castle, his brother Robert's wedding was "over, thank god, and a more depressing event I've never encountered." The bride was

Scottish, and "the Scotch and American elements of the bridal party were divided by an impassable barrier, so that we stood and stared at each other with mutual distrust." Barry didn't explain the reason for this apparent animosity. It was probably due to the Binghams' intense clan loyalty that would make any in-law unwelcome, at least initially.

Overcoming his avowed boredom, Barry had fun with his description of the event:

> The ceremony lasted hours, and I had to stand the whole time, without even kneeling during the prayers. The bride wore a fat looking dress that seems to be called a picture gown, and was built along the lines of a hogshead. Over her head she wore yards of quite heavy net, making a train which was borne by two stumbling children who kept knocking pots of ferns down.

That night, after dancing the "Strip the Willow," a Scottish reel he thought was called "Strip the Widow," Barry was "stuck with a bovine bridesmaid so I calmly ushered her to bed and began scouting around for something to do." This diversion was finally provided by two American girls and a bottle of champagne. His trials continued: "But the cork broke and I spent half an hour picking it out with a nail file. . . . I managed to keep somebody up to talk to for another couple of hours."

Finally, he was "forced to go to bed . . . damn mad not to have had a good time at my only brother's wedding, but I suppose the circumstances made it hopeless from the start."

Barry went on a side trip to London with Henrietta, and in a letter told Mary, "I went some place to dance . . . and the orchestra played 'Lantern of Love' and there I was about to weep on the tablecloth at any minute. . . . I kept thinking of the night we had dinner at the Saracen's Head when you had just gotten the music and we practiced it all during the meal."

It was a dancing age. Barry and Mary would have learned, as part of their essential social education, all the steps of the traditional ballroom dances—fox-trot, waltz, quick step—as well as the newer and flashier versions of swing, and even some suggestive Latin numbers—samba, cha-cha, perhaps even tango—and of course the Charleston. The nightclubs they frequented counted good dance music as a prerequisite as important as drink; the handsome couple would have been joined on the floor by young people dancing the Lindy Hop (a precursor to the jitterbug), as well as waltzers from their parents' generation. Over the course of their courtship, they developed, as a couple, a passion for ballroom dancing, its moods and patterns, its romantic lyrics and romantic music, as well as a polished performance style that gave them both a good deal of satisfaction.

But in 1927's fading summer, separated from her by an ocean, Barry was planning to place a transatlantic call to Mary around August 30: "Darling, for the love of heaven don't let your phone get out of order . . . because if you do I'll be shouting blasphemies and curses over long distance." He was living "for the morning of the 3rd of September, in New Haven or New London or wherever it turns out to be" where they would meet. He wanted to know if she still loved him. Rereading her letters, he remarks, was such an indulgence that

> I'm afraid those letters will never be found in a yellowed condition by some member of a future generation. I take them out and look at them so often that they will drop to pieces before any great length of time has passed.

Mary's letters may have, but Barry's didn't drop to pieces, nor did I find these particular letters in the blue box. Instead, they repose in an archive at the Filson Historical Society in Louisville. Toward the end of her life, Mary must have decided which of Barry's letters from this period she wanted to donate to the Filson as a public record of his passion, and which she chose to preserve in the blue box. Her reasoning for either choice is open to interpretation, as it was not recorded in either place.

•

In September, back in the United States after his summer abroad, Barry visited Mary at Hopkinton and then went to Boston, where he met a friend "staying at the Harvard Club, so I came along with him. We've had quite a good time, since the bar maid downstairs, age about sixty and weight about two hundred, is one of our best friends." He brought the woman "an execrable pendant" from London and in gratitude, "she's done nothing but shake up cocktails for us ever since." If he had brought Mary a present from London, he didn't mention it.

Remembering the previous week, which he and Mary spent together, he was filled "with an overwhelming sense of gratitude to Mildred for having made it possible for us to be together." He wondered if Mary remembered

> the sunset at Goffsville, or paddling around the pond after water lilies, or the stars at night at Ramon's house? I'll never see the glint of sun on pine needles again without thinking of a place in the woods up above Overnight Porches. I've said and said again that we are like people in a novel or a musical comedy, living a sort of idealized life.

Barry's next letter, written on Harvard letter paper sometime in the fall of 1927, announced that he "had to get out of town over the holiday and enjoy God's great outdoors. . . . I'm starting right away,

Warren is going with me, and we're heading up to New Hampshire."
He didn't invite Mary, although "it would be so perfectly proper, if the
Radcliffe authorities were omniscient and sympathetic to boot." He
seemed to imply that if the authorities had understood the nature of
their relationship, they would have approved.

At Christmas, he went to visit his Aunt Sadie in Asheville, where
"violent alarums and excursions" delayed his letter-writing. Aunt Mary,
Sadie's sister, joked that she had fallen downstairs in her "hurry to get
to town to a bargain sale; she and Aunt Sadie had been fallen women
all their lives." When he wrote, they were all sitting in Aunt Mary's
room—she had sprained both ankles—making Christmas presents,
looking like they "were lifted from the pages of Louisa May Alcott.
Each Little Man and Little Woman had something special to work on"
while the aunts told hilarious stories.

Barry slept in the "finest big bed with a feather mattress, and an
open fire burning in the next room." Aunt Sadie's house had no central
heating.

"I've never gotten over feeling like a little child visiting Asheville,"
he explained. "It always surprises everybody there when I realize I'm
over nine"—implying not that his family believed he was still a child,
but that he did.

"Just for variety" he went to "one wild party" in a friend's basement
"that is fixed up like a bar in Montmartre." They drank "the worst
liquor there I ever saw, but it has its effect—raw corn whiskey."

Back in Louisville, he found friends making "veiled hints at
matrimony" and one couple had secretly married. He was forthright
with Mary about his feelings on the subject, writing, "I haven't seen
them yet, but I feel so sorry for them that I feel like I'll have to nurse
them. They're so much in love they can't think what they are doing" but
soon, he predicted, they would realize they didn't even have enough
money to go to the movies. But then the groom's mother, instead of

being dismayed, wrote them a congratulatory check and the couple threw a party.

He was trying half-heartedly to accept his brother's new wife, still unnamed; Aunt Sadie had said that to her disappointment she found she actually liked her.

Hoping for a letter from Mary, he complained that he could not imagine her at "this unnatural Eastman House" where she had moved from her dormitory:

> While you were still at Bertram I felt as though I still had some connection with you, because at least I am familiar with the table in the hall, and the clock, and the four corners of the living room.

He laid out his plan to introduce her to his father on his January visit to Boston.

No account of the meeting remains.

•

At the beginning of her senior year, Mary, at the advice of one of her professors, submitted a paper comparing Aristophanes to W. S. Gilbert, which she had written for a previous year's course, to *The Classical Journal* in Lawrence, Kansas. One of the journal's editors turned it down politely: "We feel its subject would not interest as many of our readers as would others we might select." It would be many decades before she tried again to publish; she kept none of her papers from her senior year.

In her junior year, she had been asked by the Radcliffe administration, ever sensitive to bad publicity, to respond to an article published in a 1927 issue of *Harper's* titled "The Lazy Thirties" by Margaret Culkin Banning, a Radcliffe graduate. Banning wrote that

> these women between thirty and forty are on the margins of
> the decade itself. They are younger than women of that age have
> ever been before, more confident of retaining their beauty, less
> burdened by housewifery, and better educated, [yet] never have
> there been young women who were more completely addicted to
> doing just what they please.

She asserted that these women did not support the organizations their
mothers or grandmothers founded—such as the Richmond Woman's
Club—and that they "are for the most part not the women who sought
or gained the vote, but they have it without effort," and hardly bothered
to take advantage of it. Social "causes sweep by them unheeded." She
could have been describing Mary Caperton.

Banning claimed her subjects were "super-conscientious" mothers
who smothered their smaller broods with attention. They had less
"domestic help" than their mothers, but they no longer entertained
houseguests for weeks on end and nearly everyone ate in restaurants.
She concluded, "The important things in their lives are the financial
and social hierarchies. These things are as tangible to them as clubs and
causes are not."

Mary's riposte was published in the July 1927 issue of the Radcliffe
newsletter, its author identified as an undergraduate "whose writing
has already won favorable comment." In her article, Mary seems to
agree with Banning; she mercilessly lampoons her classmates—but
for their ignorance rather than their lack of a social conscience. She
writes that Radcliffe's dormitory dinner table conversation is limited
to remarks such as "My ignorance of European politics is abysmal"
or "I once read a book on Lenin by Tolstoy." When, as reported in
her essay, Mary tries to "raise the conversation to greater heights," a
classmate admits, "I simply don't have the background" for such an
elevated discourse, while a friend agrees, "I'm perfectly barbarous."

Mary concludes that her classmates are "tumultuous and titanic at least about themselves," hastening to condemn the excessive attention they've received from their parents as well as "ruinous publicity," all part of a "general primitivistic movement." This movement, Mary claims, values adolescence more than maturity, and has certainly forgotten the importance of roots, in both the grammatical and social senses of the word.

Next she describes a strange incident. While walking down a Cambridge street, whistling "in a genteel way," she hears a passerby, an older woman, muttering, "Half the girls now ought to be locked up."

"Why?" Mary shrieks, and is told, "Because they're in a pathological state, and ought to be kept under lock and key."

Mary then contrasts this woman's "passion and bitter intolerance" with "the almost inert acceptance of people and things" she abhors in her classmates.

"Standards have become vague and wavering," she asserts, because of "the break in the stream of tradition."

To drive her point home, she concludes her story later at the dormitory diner table, when she asks a classmate if she is pathological. The girl is totally engaged by her vanilla ice cream with chocolate sauce and doesn't reply.

Far from defending Radcliffe students from Banning's criticism, she went Banning one further, claiming that her classmates were worse than simply younger versions of Banning's subjects. Her complaint is not that they aren't engaged in the fates of those who are worse off, it is that they do not think of themselves as comprising society's higher echelons and therefore valuing their education. Banning's article addresses the absence of a social conscience among privileged white women; Mary lambastes her peers for their stupidity.

Richmond rules continued to influence Mary's behavior as well as her attitudes. Although she had shortened her skirts and bobbed her

hair, she seldom wore revealing dresses or makeup. She didn't drive
a fast car (she couldn't afford one), drink much (at this point in her
life), stay out late at nightclubs, or perform daring feats like those that
were beginning to define the era's New Woman: swimming the English
Channel like Gertrude Ederle in 1926, winning two Olympic gold
medals in tennis in 1924 like Helen Wills, or flying across an ocean like
Amelia Earhart in 1928. She never mentioned these women's triumphs,
which were given a great deal of attention in the press. She might have
dismissed them as novel forms of showing off. Nor does she mention
suffrage or the effect on her young life of finally receiving the vote.

Instead she was concerned with her struggle to improve the
appearance, literally, of her papers, noting sorrowfully in one letter,
"This is a specimen of the sort of work this old typewriter puts out"—
uneven, blurred, hardly up to her standards in the days before Wite-
Out and correcting ribbon. She had no money for a newer model.

In her senior year, she came under the influence of classics professor
Charles Burton Gulick. He found her paper on the Greek playwright
Menander "interesting and instructive" but felt it needed "filling
out." Their relationship quickly became affectionate; he remained her
academic mentor during the rest of her time at Radcliffe.

•

After their summer apart, Barry and Mary's September reunion in
Cambridge in the fall of 1927 was joyful. There was no further talk
of detaching. When separated from Mary, Barry used his letters to
continue to promise love in flowery terms, as well as a lot of fun, but
since they were seldom separated, these letters are fewer. At some
point, he began to define their relationship as a passionate friendship.

Since Mary kept none of the essays or bluebooks from her senior
year, it is difficult to assess how she was using her time, or how

important the college curriculum remained to her. Certainly Barry was a major distraction; he could afford to amuse himself in nightclubs, speakeasies, and restaurants in Cambridge and Boston—which Mary could never afford—while catching up on schoolwork during weekends away, which, again, she could not afford. The difference in the outcomes of their academic careers seems predictable. Mary earned only a Cum Laude degree, in spite of her early promise, while Barry— benefiting from great natural ability and the perks of privilege—was given a Magna Cum Laude.

They graduated in June 1928. With no plans for life after June, either with Barry or alone, Mary—with characteristic verve—had applied for the Charles Eliot Norton Fellowship, encouraged to do so by Professor Gulick. This prestigious fellowship offers a postgraduate year at the American School of Classical Studies in Athens. While she was completing her fellowship application, her friends were showing off engagement rings and planning June weddings.

The Norton fellowship usually led to further study and a Ph.D., followed by a life teaching Classics, as had been the case with the only other female scholar to win it, Hetty Goldman, nineteen years earlier.

But Goldman was an entirely different young woman. Born to German-Jewish parents in New York in 1881, Goldman graduated from Bryn Mawr and then studied at Radcliffe. In 1910, she published her first article, "The Orestia of Aeschylus as Illustrated in Greek Vase Painting." The article helped her win the Norton Fellowship and she studied in Athens until 1912. She then became director of archeology at Harvard's Fogg Museum, and later, the first woman to be appointed professor at the Institute of Advanced Study at Princeton.

Well-published and much-lauded, Hetty Goldman might have served as a model for Mary Caperton; in the pinch, however, the shape of Goldman's life was too unfamiliar—Goldman was Jewish, from an intellectual tradition unknown to Mary; she was outside the social pale, from Richmond's point of view; beyond her field, Mary would have thought she enjoyed little status; her income would have been meager in Mary's eyes, and, perhaps worst of all, she never married.

More subtle differences between the two women emerged after Mary won the fellowship, which Professor Gulick announced, with great pride, in March 1928. As a daughter of one of the self-proclaimed First Families of Virginia, Mary expected to find her way smoothed by friends and a powerful mentor.

Mary's fellowship at the American School was to begin in the fall of 1928. That summer, with her sister Sarah, Mary set out for Athens, stopping on the way in London. Barry turned up there with a group of friends, including Edie Callahan, a confidante who, like Barry's friend Warren Buckler, reappeared frequently in his letters and throughout his life.

Years later, Mary reminisced about Edie, saying:

> She was ageless, you know. She was one of the ugliest women in the world, [but] she was so full of charm and sympathy and outgoingness. . . . She was a Catholic for one thing and she had a great faith in the second life which I didn't have.

Edie was one of Barry's earliest friends, and she never lost a special place in his affections. During the last years of her life, she would live in a house he had built for her across from the Big House outside Louisville.

Barry also brought along his friends Francis Parks and Warren; Mary may not have expected the entourage. Barry entreated her in a note, "Darling, I just found out at lunch time where you were, after a wild goose chase by telephone all over London. Sweetheart, will you go to the theatre and prance around with me tonight?"

In London, Mary and Sarah entered into a round of nightclubbing and theatre-going. They were often out most of the night; at the end of her life, Mary remembered a recurring scene when Edie would plead at her mother's locked hotel room door at four a.m., "Mudie, it's me, let me in." "And then," Mary remembered, Edie's mother "would come raging to the door."

In August, Mary and Sarah left London to visit their great aunts, Mary and Minna Lefroy, in Sussex; the visit was not a success. The constraints Sallie and Helena had so easily accepted were no longer imaginable to these young women. Mary long remembered her aunts' rules during their visit:

> Of course we couldn't smoke. We used to disappear to the far end
> of the garden and smoke and they were so old and sort of fragile,
> they ate very little. So we were really very hungry a great deal of
> the time.
> We devised a scheme that we would take a bus into the
> neighboring village where there was a library.

They would tell Aunt Minna that they had run out of books and were planning to have lunch while they were in the village, which produced the much-desired respite:

> Well, they were very reluctantly letting us out of their sight. . . .
> Then we would lapse into a pub and eat quantities of sausage and
> drink beer. And then we would go back in a much better frame
> of mind.

In spite of the girls' dissatisfaction, old family ties between the Irish and American families still held; at her death, Aunt Minna left a ten-thousand-dollar trust fund for the benefit of Helena and her children.

In London, Mary and Sarah stayed with another Lefroy aunt and uncle, since putting up at a hotel would have been out of the question.

Again, their days were "absolutely circumscribed, we couldn't do anything without one of them coming along with us." About to leave for the Isle of Wight, Mary asked her hosts if she might

> invite my friend Barry Bingham to come for the weekend. . . . And I think it scared them terribly. Barry did come and then when we would go to bathe Uncle Ted would insist on going with us and he had the most obscene bathing suit, what do they call them, bathing dresses and no jock strap. And it was all very loose hanging.

In her remembrances, Mary did not appear to have been particularly shocked by the display.

In September, the friends gathered in Paris, where they all signed the menu from Le Dôme in Montparnasse; its slogan was "Ouvert Toute La Nuit." Later, Barry dropped Mary a note from the Hôtel Napoléon, "Mary Darling, Rumplemayer's at 1 o'clock, if I'm still alive by then." It was all a flattering whirl, and the fellowship and Athens must have seemed very far away.

Barry and Sarah, along with Barry's traveling companions, then escorted Mary to Athens where she was due to register at the American School at the end of September.

Founded in 1881 by nine American universities, housed in an impressive group of buildings in the middle of Athens, the School sponsored a dig at Corinth and in the Athenian Agora and operated two important research libraries. Its purpose was, and is, serious: to train future academics and archeologists. But the school had room, at least in the 1920s, for more casual students, arranging tours where the archeologists pursued their mission with help from the other fellows, who also engaged in a good deal of sightseeing, swimming, and picnicking.

Barry and his merry band stayed on in Athens after Mary registered, continuing their late-night carousing; Mary joined them in their revelry and at one point, perhaps unwisely, invited them to visit her room. By October, the authorities at the Academy were complaining that Mary was seldom on campus and was causing a scandal by spending her evenings in Athens' bars.

On October 22, Professor Gulick, who had recommended her for the fellowship, wrote to Mary of his "keen disappointment and bitter grief" over reports of her behavior. The report he received from the on-site professor, a man named Carpenter,

> has made me feel that the Committee has made a grave mistake in conferring the Fellowship on you. Dr. Carpenter says you have violated nearly every rule he has laid down, and that your attitude towards teachers and students is marked by discourtesy and aloofness.

Professor Gulick had cabled Carpenter that he supported "any measures he took for the good of the school," and subsequently advised Mary that

> if he [Carpenter] will condone what you have done, you should make full apology to him and to Mrs. Carpenter, agree to place yourself entirely under her guidance in all social matters, and settle down at once to the serious and regular business which was entrusted to you. You must keep out of nightclubs entirely. . . . You may not act as an ordinary tourist in an ordinary city; even if you were such you would have to remember that in Athens the behavior of American girls—to us wholly innocent—is not understood and is constantly criticized; that servants talk freely and start malicious rumors. It was madness for you to have boys

in your room in Athens when you know that would not be tolerated at Radcliffe.

Whether you like the people there or not is beside the question, but if on reflection you find that you do not like the work and the prospect of a year in Athens, you must resign at once and come home.

I am still hoping that what I have written to Dr. Carpenter may determine him to give you another chance.

Signing himself, "Affectionately, Charles Burton Gulick," he added in a postscript, "I have held this letter several days hoping to hear from you but nothing has come."

Rather than apologizing, Mary defended herself aggressively. She had escaped the strictures and oversight of her family that summer only to find that the academic world, even abroad, was equally concerned with enforcing correct and, always, ladylike behavior. Nine letters in the blue box detail this contretemps. She never mentioned in her oral history the events these letters detail, and the story never appeared in family lore. Apparently no one, not even Barry, knew what had happened.

In her letter of November 5 to Gulick, she wrote with a

burning sense of injustice and bewilderment, and I must take up in detail statements in your letter which I can neither understand nor for which I can find justification in my conduct.

You tell me that Mr. Carpenter says that I have "violated nearly every rule which he has laid down" and that my "attitude toward teachers and students is marked by discourtesy and aloofness." In the first place, I can think of no definite rules which Mr. Carpenter laid down for me. . . . The criticism of my attitude of "discourtesy and aloofness" is distressingly vague, but I assure you that I have

behaved toward no one in the school with any conscious rudeness,
or in a way at all different from my usual manner, with which I
think you are sufficiently well acquainted to judge. You tell me
that I should make a full apology to Mr. and Mrs. Carpenter and
I am at a loss to know for what to apologize. I "must stay out of
nightclubs entirely." I have never been to a nightclub in Athens. I
did not even know that there were any there.

Beneath the concerns over reputation and compliance lurked the
issue of Mary's drinking. This had hardly been a factor during her first
years at Radcliffe, but as soon as she began to see Barry, she was drawn
into his heavy consumption of alcohol at college parties and in speakeasies. She said later that their drinking, which Prohibition had made
illegal, was first and foremost a rebellion against authority. Since this
rebellion was not expressed in any other way, it seems likely that Barry
was by the end of his college career a serious alcoholic and that Mary
was coming along not far behind him. Certainly she knew there were
nightclubs in Athens since, according to their letters, they were where
she and Barry and his friends were spending most of their evenings.

In her defense, she explained to Gulick what had happened the
night of the incident with Carpenter:

Edith and Barry and Francis came up to the school to see me.
Edith wanted to see my room to discuss interior decoration and
we all went up together. Mr. Carpenter passed by in the hall and
came in to tell me that the reception room was downstairs, and I
explained to him exactly what was taking place and then we left
immediately.

Mary went on to protest the implications inherent in Carpenter's
complaint:

I think the harshest and most undiscriminating construction must have been put on [the visit] since you write me that it was "madness for me to have boys in my room"—the innuendo is very shocking and painful to me—and considering, as I do in this case, that Edith Callahan was more or less in loco parentis, I would hardly have expected such a construction from the Radcliffe authorities themselves had the same thing taken place in Bertram Hall.

In the middle of this contretemps, Barry and his entourage left Athens. He went to visit his sister Henrietta in Switzerland before going home to begin writing a novel.

A few days after Barry's departure, Mary wrote Helena—"Mother darling"—and sent her a copy of Gulick's letter. She pleaded with her mother, "Please don't let it get outside the family. I haven't even written Barry about it as it would only make him uselessly uncomfortable." Mary confided:

It has been, to put it mildly, perfect hell until I got the whole thing more or less straightened out. . . . I am still amazed by the smallness of the whole thing, and I feel that I have been unfairly treated. My first impulse was to resign the Fellowship.

She told Helena that when she confronted Carpenter with Gulick's letter, Carpenter insisted that he did not write the accusations. Eventually Mary found out that his assistant, Mr. Luce, wrote the incriminating details to Gulick, and things then became very difficult for the unfortunate Luce. After Mary revealed the source of the rumor, Gulick wrote that he had always known Luce "to be a jackass," and that he would "make it very hot for him" if he continued to stir up trouble.

As for Dr. Carpenter, his only complaint was that Mary had misunderstood "the attitude toward American girls" in Athens, and that her behavior had caused the servants to gossip. Mary responded to this amended concern, writing to Gulick:

> I do not feel particularly culpable in not having understood the attitude. . . . Nothing which I have met in my experience has prepared me for it and I do not feel that my behavior would be open to criticism in any civilized country. As for the servants, I cannot help a tearful grin. I have never been brought up to model my conduct upon the ideas of etiquette of people of this class.

Now Helena wrote a furious letter to Gulick, defending her daughter's honor, and he replied that he and his wife shared her "burning indignation." She must have asked him to seek some sort of restitution, for he warned her that if he did so the whole affair would become public, but at this point, "No one knows anything." He pleaded with her to persuade Mary not to resign the Fellowship, insisting that he remained "thoroughly proud of her." His change in attitude is hard to understand, unless Mary's fierce defense of her conduct persuaded him.

After all this, Mary felt that her position at the Academy was "insecure and strange." She was particularly upset because the episode might have undermined Gulick's friendship, but he assured her this was not so—"Radcliffe is not Radcliffe without Mary"—signing himself, "Uncle Charles."

By December 14 Mary wrote her mother, "The whole affair has more or less blown over." The Carpenters invited her to dinner, an invitation that she accepted, though the experience was not "particularly hilarious or agreeable."

Now she pounced on Luce, the bearer of bad news, as "hopelessly dull and sort of backwoods provincial New England"; she heard a rumor that Dr. Carpenter had threatened to resign his post as director of the school if the committee "reappoints Mr. Luce—and the grounds for his saying this are largely on account of this affair of mine."

Her letters of rebuttal reveal a willingness to fudge the facts, as when she claimed she didn't even know there were nightclubs in Athens. Her consciousness of her own righteousness never wavered—there was never a chance that she would apologize—but apparently she didn't tell Barry about the episode, which might have shed an unflattering light on his would-be fiancée.

The spat highlights Mary's determination to protect her options; she had no intention of curtailing her relationship with Barry, nor would she abandon the Norton Fellowship. They were officially adults now, Radcliffe's parietal rules and Richmond's conventions left behind, and she intended to live her own life and to have fun with as few consequences as possible.

She continued to view Dr. Carpenter and his wife as "blots on the landscape," reluctantly admitting that he did give a good lecture on "the archaic things in the museum," and she refused to speak to Luce or to attend his lectures. Both men were authorities in their field, and Carpenter's work at Corinth was particularly important; he discovered Greek and Roman graves and a church from the age of Justinian. His overriding belief that "We must insist on the old faith of the Humanists in the humanities (and not the pre-human-ites, or even the exhuman-ites)" dovetailed nicely with Mary's prejudices and her love of the elevated tradition, but she did not overcome her antipathy.

In December 1928, she looked forward to Christmas celebrations at the school, which included charades organized by the wife of the school's librarian. She writes Helena, "Really, don't be blasé, they are the most antiquated and suburban London things in the world. And Mrs. Scroggin is the most chirrupy round little thing with a continual worm in her beak and her parties are very funny."

In Athens, Mary was befriended by Zora Stephens, a diplomat's wife from California, who played an increasingly important role in her life. Mary admired Zora's clothes, her worldliness, and her money, describing her as "very attractive—a beautifully groomed thin-legged Californian who has lived all over the place."

Zora's husband, Dorsey Stephens, "is out here manipulating a loan for the Greek government." His role at a time of violent economic and political disruptions in Greece was not of great interest to Mary, who in her letters was seemingly unaware of the coups and countercoups taking place in Athens. Rather than comment on these events, she asked Helena to send her a set of jersey silk underwear for Christmas.

As the gloomy Greek winter closed in, she wrote Barry that she was lonely and homesick. She didn't mention her courses or her reading. A family myth I'd never questioned held that at some point that winter, after reading Mary's complaints about the cold and her loneliness, Barry went to Greece to fetch her, bringing the fellowship year to an abrupt close. He used to describe with great amusement the voyage back across the north Atlantic in a wild winter storm, making everyone seasick except for Barry and Mary. In fact, she insisted on playing her violin every evening with the ship's orchestra (the only time I ever heard of her playing) with, according to Barry, terrible screeching of the strings. Perhaps that was the reason she never played the violin again.

Now it seemed the Charles Eliot Norton Fellowship, considered such a plum—she outdistanced four men to win it—had lost its luster. Possibly she felt that after their summer together Barry was close to making a commitment, and so other options were less attractive. But Barry planned to spend the winter in Asheville with his Aunt Sadie. He wanted to finish his novel, the opening salvo of his literary career.

He began that winter to save some of Mary's letters. On an outing to Delphi, she wrote:

My sweet, you must come here sometime—with me, I hope, because now I can be very illuminating about daubs and peep-holes and the very complicated question about the dates of the different treasuries. The survey has really got me back to a more normal frame of mind, and I feel, what I did not until I got here, that I can live through the winter.

This afternoon I sat up in the theatre of Dionysus and watched a sunset which was full of that Perugino luminosity of colors—a strange bluish green—and a clarity and coolness in the air—you know, so that the faraway cries of small birds seem quite close. Nothing breaks the sort of abstract stillness and calm of the place but the sound of the donkeys' bells and the peasant women's distant upbraidings. Then, later, when the last light is dying out the reflection lies in long streamers over the hills. The whole place seems inviolable. Perhaps it is some childhood psychological association, but I think that as the Psalms say our strength comes from the everlasting hills.

•

By January 1929, Barry had failed to send Mary a Christmas present; his sister Henrietta, rubbing salt into the wound, cabled her in Athens: "I hope Barry's Christmas present arrives." The oversight, Barry wrote in his next letter, "makes me want to breathe forth flames and brimstone," but no present appeared.

"What special kind of studying are you doing, Dearest?" he asked. Mary replied in March:

I have been working at a restoration of the west porch of the Propylean, that is, trying to identify the architrave blocks which are scattered among the debris all over the Acropolis. Francis

> Capps and I are doing it together and spend hours running
> around with meter sticks measuring blocks and earnestly putting
> down the results. It's rather fun.

She was also drawing plans for the roofing of the porch and included
a sketch: "Mine looked something like this. Everybody was properly
mystified."

Mary's letters gave few other details beyond a vague "I think there
will be courses," after the group of students returned from touring the
Greek islands. The tour was the high point of her first semester; she sent
Barry the journal she kept in a small blue notebook: visiting ruins, eating and drinking, swimming and sunbathing in the nude with the other
women. He must have returned it to her later; I found it in the blue box.

In Georgia, at his father's hunting lodge, Barry had almost finished
his novel:

> I don't believe the rewriting will be so bad, because strange to
> say it is written straight out with very few mixed-up places and I
> don't believe I can do much beyond plain copying.

He passed his handwritten draft to a cadre of secretaries, hired by
his father, although he was embarrassed to have them read his work,
writing to Mary, "There are parts that I know are very trashy." (He
added that they didn't seem much interested.) After Barry sent her one
of his sonnets, Mary replied in her next note:

> I'm so pleased that you sent it. I am densely ignorant about
> poetry in general and metrical ones in particular, but the pace
> of this seems to suit the mood of Sirmion, remarkably. And of
> all the places in Greece, except the Nike Temple, this is the one I
> associate with you most closely.

Then she asked him not to repudiate the sonnet's sentiments because he wrote it when he had a hangover.

Mary's letters during the spring of 1929 were mostly about her social life in Athens. Zora Stephens, she wrote,

> gave a dinner party and it was very exciting because of the presence of the Greek prime minister, frail looking, has a white head, and thin quick sensitive hands. . . . Zora told him, with some exaggeration, that I was an archeologist, and he peered across the table round the flowers and laughed out loud and said, "But I thought they always had long beards!"

Then they all went dancing and "I got home at four o'clock and got up at seven to go to Marathon with the School." On the way back,

> Rachel Sargent with whom I was walking got something the matter with her hip. She is very funny—an old maid from Mayorsville, wherever that may be, who is writing a treatise on Greek slavery. We came upon a man loading wood into a cart and Rachel accosted him and asked him, in Greek, to unload the wood and drive us. . . . He said he would love to, but his women were up on the hill and they wouldn't like it. But finally we found one with less violently monogamous convictions and we climbed in and rattled along.

Meanwhile Barry had left on another family trip. Mary wrote,

> I was so amused and delighted to get your adorable letter all about your travels in the Far West. I must say, going about like that en masse sounds very nice, you know, friendly and cheerful and surrounded by all the dear ones at home.

After complimenting Barry on his family, Mary presented him with an entertaining story about a mishap-laden jaunt of her own. She wrote that she had

> the strangest week you ever heard of. The Stephens invited me to go with Ed Pinney, the lawyer from Seligman's, to see something in Greece. We decided to go to Delphi, although it was snowing a little, even in Athens, and took the Simplon, meaning to go as far as Bralo and there be met by a car. . . . We started out with all the sweaters, coats, and blankets we could assemble, Huntley and Palmer's assorted biscuits, whiskey and brandy and some New Yorkers.

At Bralo, they had found themselves completely snowed in and, so,

> decided to go on up the line as far as Larissa and catch the Simplon coming down. The further north we went the more violent the storm became, and finally after one of those long insidious train drinking sessions accompanied by variations of bridge and Russian Bank, we staggered off at Larissa.

While waiting for a train, due to pass through at midnight,

> we went to a little hotel and ordered a room and a fire. All the villagers seated around the stove were firmly convinced that we were coming to Larissa from Athens for four hours . . . for no good. They probably thought it was some kind of curious hasty American assignation.

In the room—

typical of Greek gracious instinct, about nine by twelve, with a table, three chairs, three beds and a brazier, we sat down to wait. It was simply freezing and the brazier was most inadequate and there was Zora sitting up looking like something very fastidious and off the Rue de la Paix in a leopard-skin coat and square-cut diamonds, reading aloud from *The New Yorker*, which by this time was dog-eared and covered with bridge scores in the margins.

The night grew on apace and at intervals the boy would come up to say the train was an hour or two later. Finally at two o'clock we heard it would get in at five, so in our hats, gloves and fur coats we got ourselves tucked into the beds. Nobody slept, of course, and we were all in that maudlin state of exhaustion in which anything anybody says seems simply hysterically funny. (Do you remember that lunch at Rumpelmayer's the day we left Paris?) But finally I got so cold and felt so ill I said I thought I was dying and Ed kept getting up from his bed and coming over . . . and saying, "Zora, make Mary get between the blankets!" You see, I didn't trust the beds and thought it safer to stay outside.

Finally the train arrived and they made it to Athens, having never been near Delphi.

I went to the Petit Palais and had a hot bath in Zora's tub and then we all sat about in negligees and things in front of the fire and had one of those relaxed hotel bedroom scenes that we are both so fond of, with lots of hot tea and buttered toast.

Not satisfied with these delights, Ed and Dorsey insisted on going out to dance at a place called the Florida. We all have a violent crush on a woman there named Suzy Meridal who is just a born fool and as funny as the devil, and has the usual tragic and completely incongruous background with the three-year-old child and the deserting husband, and also a perfectly grand whiskey tenor that could be heard as far as the Piraeus.

Mary's adventures certainly rivaled those of the Bingham's Western tour. And her festivities continued; the School had apparently abandoned all hope of reining in the holder of the Charles Eliot Norton Fellowship.

Throughout the spring of 1929, Mary continued to regale Barry with stories of her Athenian evenings out on the town in all its guises.

Last night Zora and Dorsey and Ed and a strange young man . . . and I went to dinner and the Florida. Zora doesn't like to dance so I had to step around steadily from eleven to four and now I feel rather drawn. These dancing floors are like corduroy roads and so it is no laughing matter to keep five men properly exercised all night. Dear, dear, that sounds positively ribald. The Stephens want to fly to Constantinople next weekend, but I can't decide whether or not to go. I am still a little enfeebled [from eating "an elderly sole"] and besides I want to finish a piece of work.

This marked the last time Mary mentioned work in her letters.

Mary's forbearance from academic talk seems to have enabled one of those curious shifts that allow relationships to proceed. From this letter on, it is Barry who comments on his reading. He wrote to her:

I read *Orlando*, darling, and it gave me very little satisfaction. . . .
It seems to me that she (Virginia Woolf) had good material
for a serious book and for something like a satire on the heavily
personal biography, if she only could have had a good strong cup
of tea before she decided to write anything down and made up
her mind what she wanted to do. I should think V. Sackville-
West would consider it a very doubtful compliment to be made
the protagonist of such a book, and to have her picture put in to
boot as Orlando in the female orbit.

He added that he read *Mrs. Dalloway* in Georgia and "liked it very much
as an experimental piece of work" but much preferred *To the Lighthouse*.
He continued to read contemporary fiction for the rest of his life.

Their academic history did not entirely evaporate. After ordering a
book by one of their Harvard professors, George Kittredge, on witches
and witchcraft, Barry asked Mary:

Do you remember his burning and ill-suppressed desire to play
one of the witches in *Macbeth*, and the way he used to wave
his arms round and thrust out his beard to show us how the
prophetic words should be delivered?

A Bingham family jaunt to Baltimore was in the offing. Barry
wished he could visit Warren Buckler there, but

I sent him a foul and filthy French postcard as a Christmas
greeting and that precocious little Mary opened it before he
got there and showed it to Mama Buckler, so I imagine I'll be
forbidden the house. Warren said his father got hold of it and
considered it a great joke, and furthermore wanted to spirit it
away and add it to his collection of anatomical charts.

In return, Mary wrote that some shipboard acquaintances have shown up in Athens. He replied:

> The picture of Doris looking at the Parthenon under heavy lids in a blinding snowstorm is perfectly incongruous and absurd. I'm so glad they didn't get a chance to stay over one night, because I'm sure they would have wanted to go out to a night club to get lecherously tight and start pawing all over you.

His next paragraph—perhaps teasingly, perhaps defensively—almost urged her to experiment:

> My dearest, Crete does sound exciting. I hope you will see some of the genuine Greeks with hyacinthine locks and lovely blonde skins that are reputed to wander in the back country on that island.

It seems nothing she wrote fully aroused his jealousy; he knew she was, as she admitted, "the victim of an idée fixe." He even enthused over reports of Mary's partying.

> However exhausting those bouts are I think they make you more intensely alive . . . and the time seems absolutely endless, doesn't it, when you keep on drinking and staying up without ever giving yourself a chance of a relapse.

Then Mary wrote to him from a trip to Delos, appealing to his love of effervescence:

> We took off our clothes and went into the surf, very rough and cold. But the effect is like nothing else I can think of but a champagne cocktail in the morning after a night before.

The memory sparked another, of summers in the Virginia countryside when "Sarah and I would follow the hay rake all day to pick up the nests of baby rabbits, and when the nurse used to have to undress us and put us to bed, literally drugged with sleepiness."

Meanwhile, the five stenographers had typed Barry's manuscript: "In cold hard print it looks so childish and threadbare . . . the work of an infant," yet he forged on with his plan to publish the novel within two years of their graduation. He decided that its success or failure would seal his fate as a writer:

> I'm actually waiting here in New York for a meeting with Carl Brandt, who is supposed to run the best literary agency in town. I got here Monday morning all booted and spurred to see him.
>
> I called his office, and his secretary said he was out of town and wouldn't be back till Tuesday. I called again yesterday, and the secretary was affable and friendly, but she said that Mr. Brandt was terribly busy and wouldn't be able to see me before Monday. I then opened up on her with a long sob story about how I was waiting in New York to see him, and how I was determined to hang on until I made some disposition of my book. I got so pathetic that she began to take pity on me, evidently believing I was staking my all on this meeting. She said in a kindly tone that she would arrange an interview for me on Friday, and asked me where I was staying. I said, "The Ritz" and she cried "The Ritz!" as though she couldn't believe her ears, but anyway I have the engagement.

The meeting with Brandt was "harrowing" in spite of the agent's attempts to be tactful. After praising incidents in the novel Barry already felt were hopelessly bad, Brandt "lit into the weakness of the plot and the general slackness of the technique that made the whole thing impossible." Still, Brandt sent the manuscript to an editor at *Harper's* who then told Barry, according to a letter sent in 1929 to Mary, "There is something so horribly wrong with the novel I am advised not to attempt to rewrite it."

Titled *The Lonesome Road*, the novel's style and content would have seemed dated even in 1929; it was modeled on the popular fiction of Barry's childhood such as John Fox, Jr.'s *The Little Shepherd of Kingdom Come*, published in 1903.

The heroine of Barry's novel, seventeen-year-old Julie—with the requisite golden hair—is a mountain girl, illegitimate daughter of a mother her grandmother says was "marked by the devil" and a "streetwalker."

Julie goes to babysit for a wealthy family, the Wheatleys, who are spending the summer in the mountains, and immediately forms a bond with their imaginative little son, Cam: "He would never be sorry for Julie, or make her remember that she couldn't be happy. And so the alliance between them began."

Julie is, however, attracted to the older Wheatley son, Richard— "the tall boarding school hero"—although he is cruel to her. Richard doesn't notice that she is, as Barry writes, "The heir of two civilizations, two races that met on the fringe of the mountains. Behind her lay the heritage of the Blue Ridge Mountaineers, that tall, somber, hardy stock" who had "interbred until the race was half broken with decay." But there is also Julie's other inheritance:

> In the softness of mouth, the upward sweep from brow to hair, any observer could read her father's gentle birth. . . . At first glance, she seemed a clear-faced mountain girl; at second, she was a woman with blue blood in her veins.

Much as in Helena's fictions, Barry's characters are pawns of their heritage, which never allows them to move beyond their inherited positions in society.

The novel's most moving scene shows Julie singing her dying grandfather a mountain lullaby:

> "We are all nodding, nid nid nodding/We are all nodding and dropping off to sleep." She exhorts herself, "Not to cry! Not to cry! He is looking in your face, and singing the old melodies that belonged to youth and life. How young he looked as he sang! This must be the beginning of things, not an end."

Julie's future depends on the men she meets: Richard Wheatley, who seduces her in the woods—in this world, since she is a prostitute's daughter, she can only resist for so long—then tells everyone that he was not the first; Mark Clemons, a mountain man who asks her to marry him—"He was big and clumsy as a bear!"; her kindly neighbor, Joe, who proposes to her, promising, "If we ever have children, I'll make it the object of my life to see that they have a fair chance for happiness."

But Joe leaves for New York to seek his fortune, and Julie, who's pregnant with Richard's child, decides to marry the bearlike Mark for the sake of her child; he agrees, but when their house burns down, Julie miscarries, and the Wheatley's little boy, Cam, pops up in the woods to offer her a sort of salvation. They both know, he tells her, how to escape into fantasy.

For all its melodrama, the novel sometimes gleams with descriptions of mountain woods and hollows, drawn from Barry's love of the countryside around Asheville. But it was, as he knew, impossible for an audience reading Hemingway, Faulkner, and Fitzgerald.

In the wake of the *Harper's* rejection, Barry mourned in a letter to Mary, "I feel terribly aimless and idle now and really don't know what I'm going to do with myself until I begin plugging away at the *Courier-Journal*"—his father's Louisville newspaper. He filled the next three weeks with nonstop partying and theatre-going in New York; his father was paying the bills.

Mary was perturbed by the fate of Barry's novel, writing him from Athens in May 1929:

> I'm sorry about the novel. A perfectly hypothetical guess on my part makes me think that in it you were trying to get back to plot (and you know Aristotle said the mythos, or plot, was the chief thing of all) away from the subjective emotional excess that all literature is sinking into. I should think, granting that this is the case, that Mr. Brandt's and the other readers' criticism might make you grind your teeth. Why is rewriting it out of the question? Of course, not having read it it's very foolish of me to go on jabbering like this, but sweetheart, what I do feel is that you had a theory that you would devote this year to writing and that your whole subsequent career as a writer would have to stand or fall on the success or failure of this one piece of work. Isn't that rather precipitous?

But it was too late; Barry had already given up.

He wrote to Mary that he had three blind dates in one weekend. He'd gone to a dance at Smith College where "horrible little hussies" kept breaking in on him without waiting to be introduced. He reported driving back to New York drunk in an open car in a snowstorm.

Mary paid him back in kind with descriptions of a "Mr. MacGregor" she had met in Athens who represented "immense finesse and hyper civilization . . . fascinating . . . highly illuminating and delightful," although, she admitted, he made her feel like "a wild Indian shrieking on the plains of Colorado."

She was delighted to hear that Barry had gone to see her sister Harriette performing in a New York nightclub with her longstanding dance partner, Vernon Biddle. Barry wrote, "She stopped the show. . . . With any sort of luck Hattie should go to the top in musical comedies."

But, Mary reported, Helena had written in a "too too silken way" about Vernon's suitability: "Philadelphia Biddle indeed! He's common as dirt, and she knows it as well as I do." Mary disparaged a photograph of "Harriette crouching down in that lascivious way, actually inviting criminal assault," and was only partly mollified by a cable from Helena insisting that the partnership was only professional and that photographs and gossip were a necessary part of "the business."

Warm spring weather had finally arrived in Greece, and Mary often went swimming in the Aegean with other women students. She described these jaunts, and her compatriots, to Barry: "Algie . . . in the nude, extraordinarily brown and attractive." Barry replied that Mary must look like one of Neptune's nymphs rising from the foam, improved by an "all-over natural tan."

By May, she was planning her return home, although the Academy expected her to stay until the end of the semester on June 15, 1929. But, she confided to Barry, "If the thought of last spring and the spring before in Cambridge makes you feel lonely and homesick, Sweetest, it makes me feel as though I've been left alone on Mars."

She had learned by then not to crowd him, writing that "In a moment of frenzy I decided that I would go to London and Paris before coming home. God knows why, as the only thing I really want is to see you, and as soon as possible." Barry hadn't committed to meeting her ship. Perhaps she felt a little more independence would lure him.

Still, she could not resist trying to make plans for him. Mildred Penn, at home in New Hampshire, had invited Mary to visit, adding in her "impersonal and languid way that she wished I would bring some beaux. . . . If you don't mind putting yourself in that category, I wish to God you'd come and meet me in New York and go to Hopkinton."

She realized that Barry became more attentive when she seemed to be slipping away, and so she wrote him from Paris on June 29 about an American Express official who took her to the boat train "and stood kissing my hand and saying loudly in French that he would miss me. Then I picked up an Englishman and had dinner with him."

It didn't work. Barry was on a family vacation in California when Mary's boat docked in New York. Terribly disappointed, she complained that she had "a horrible foreboding that you will go to Scotland for the grouse hunting and we will not see each other at all."

Left in the lurch, she had to find a job or face going back to Richmond. Mildred Penn again arranged for her to work in a teashop in Concord, New Hampshire. Mary always remembered how generously Mildred "more or less adopted me, giving me clothes and the chance to make a few dollars babysitting."

If Mary wrote to Barry that summer, he did not keep the letters, and apparently they did not see each other.

By the fall of 1929, the teashop where she had been employed was closing. Mary worked hard to find a job in Boston and was appointed assistant to the advertising manager at the publishing company Little, Brown. She rented an apartment on Irving Street with another Radcliffe graduate, Constance Templeton.

Other friends from college were lingering in Boston; Mary cooked dinner for Barry's friends—hers as well since the previous summer's travels—Francis Parks and Warren Buckler. Warren wrote his mother in November 1929:

> Mary has finally gotten herself an excellent job with Little, Brown the publisher and is now happily settled for the winter. She has really developed a tremendous depth of character and is about as fine as any girl I know. I didn't realize what a fine head she has until her employers began to flatter her. . . . They can't believe that any girl could pay so much attention to her clothes and her appearance and have any intelligence at all. . . . I am told they sit in mute amazement and watch Mary do a hard day's work

in an intriguing Paris creation and high-heeled shoes. . . . Her chief job is to interview various writers either personally or by mail so as to write the blurbs that appear on all the new books the company publishes.

Mary is the one person I've seen among my contemporaries to whom maturity seems a blessing. Instead of just getting dull and conventional as so many of my friends have, she is getting more wide awake and interested in the current of life around her.

But then, as Warren noted,

Barry descends upon us with a trunk load of Kentucky Bourbon and with a lust for turning us all into mad satyrs and fauns and dervishes. I have been waddling about after him ever since like Sancho Panza, breathless and amazed. He is having his last fling before settling down to work, which I think will be very good for him.

Warren went on,

He has developed very little in the last year. He hasn't acquired the serene balance of mind that comes with maturity as Mary has, and I simply can't understand why he doesn't take her to wife, because I think she would be the most wonderful and steadying influence on him. But he is still just playing with the bait in the old way, and Mary like a true angler is very patient. But I think it is hurting her much more than she ever dares to let on. But Barry's great charm is that he is the eternal ingénue, and I think he wants to maintain that pose as long as his youth holds out.

At the end of her life, Mary remembered Barry's visits to Boston, one of which lasted six weeks, as "very disruptive." During what she called "this emotional time," she became more and more unhappy with their relationship. She feared that it was deteriorating into something "sordid." She refused to be like her roommate, Constance Templeton, who was taking graduate courses, but "her real interest, it seemed to me, was her lover," to the point that Mary had to leave the apartment so she could entertain him. (Constance went on to earn an AB at Oxford in 1930, apparently unimpeded by her love life.) Mary recalled:

> I really thought it was awful, that he was treating her terribly.
> You know, gentlemen simply didn't seduce young ladies in those
> days. Barry never tried to seduce me, though I imagine at several
> points he could have quite easily.

I found few letters in the blue box from this period. In one, written in December 1929, Mary humorously imitated the tone of her beloved sixteenth-century play, *Gammer Gurton's Needle*: "I am indeed Grateful for the Enlightening and Edifying disquisition on Equitation recently arrived by packet." Her parody thanked Barry for a "Great Quantity of Roses," adding that she and Constance had been to many parties and "I feel no guilt in honestly confessing that last night we were both in our Altitudes and saw two-a-moons" before "being unbuttoned with all respect and tenderness" and put to bed "in our shifts," presumably in all innocence, by one Henry Smith.

She closed with an explanation that, after much "Turmoil of mind," she had decided not to go on a trip with "Mistress Penn and family" because it wouldn't "Enhance my reputation in the Eyes of Masters Little and Brown." She added, with a hint of a sly reprimand to Barry, "I cannot Risk appearing fantastick and wrong-headed, and I have resolv'd to settle down seriously to the Business of Life."

In return, Barry wrote to her about his own business of life, cataloguing the rigors of his new job at his father's radio station in Louisville: "I'm crowded into a cell-like room with two huge desks, a coatrack, a telephone, and one small prison window set high in the wall, not barred, but effectually obliterated by soot"—a sharp contrast to his bedroom in his Italianate villa across the lawn from his father's Big House. His job was to

> write the things the announcers say during the programs. . . .
> The more dripping the style, the more pleased are the office
> force. . . . I go on regardless of my total ignorance . . . with a
> musical dictionary close at hand.

Facing his "radio debut," he was

> scared perfectly speechless, by reading a sketch of Sidney Lanier's
> life and several other peculiar things. No first night at the
> Harvard Dramatic Club ever gave me such a gone feeling in my
> stomach.
>
> I get up at a quarter to eight, and reach the office before nine
> each morning, no matter how hard I try to delay. I have a great
> big hot breakfast on a tray in the living room, with whatever
> sunshine exists coming in through the windows, and it is all most
> cheerful. I usually get home about five-thirty in the evening to
> an open fire which never fails to help my morale. Bridge games
> in the evening are very frequent, and I'm learning the working
> person's lesson of taking one or two drinks but not a third on
> week nights.
>
> The worst feature is the lack of time for the amenities of life,
> reading, writing letters, and all that; the best feature is having
> so many small tasks to overcome and pass beyond, with the
> accompanying sensation of accomplishment. The people in the

office are all nice tacky people in glasses who are embarrassingly obliging to me.

Though he tried to blend in, he was inevitably and always seen as the owner's son.

He concluded rather formally by hoping that she was "still enjoying your job, and that you are, as I am, filled with health and spirits."

In March 1930, he was still adjusting to his life and work in Louisville, writing to Mary, "I have been as busy as a bird dog, trying to keep up with the increasing demands of this strange job and at the same time entertaining a succession of relatives," including his aunts and cousins from Asheville and his sister Henrietta, who thoroughly enjoyed taking over as "host."

He had kept up his connection not just with Mary, but also with her family. Mary's youngest sister Melinda came with her mother to visit young Helena, recently married to the four-flusher and settled in Louisville. In his March letter, Barry wished that there were something like New York's Gypsy Bar in Louisville where "Lena and your mother and I could have a grand time just among ourselves."

In the midst of his busy life, Barry wrote Mary,

> I do want to get back to Boston so badly and so far I can't even be sure that I can get away to go to New York. Francis suggests a party for all of us at the camp, followed by an evening of wholesome fun with the whiskey bottle.

Louisville nightlife "is amusing lately in an obscene way," Barry went on. "Debutantes of the season are quite calmly going the way of all flesh, people are living together who have no business doing it, and two men have even gone so far as to leave their wives and babes and go off to live with two other men."

Barry continued to use his letters to communicate a sense of *joie de vivre*, writing to Mary that he and Edie Callahan "spend our time reveling in the dirt." He included, for Mary, a four-page poem in the heroic manner on a struggle Edie had with a goose that invaded her parked car during the night; she was saved by Barry's housemaid, "the goddess Lizzie."

In another letter, he asked,

> How do you do these days? Is Mistress Constance Templeton still gracing your abode with her genteel presence? I'd give anything to see you both in all your blondness sipping mint juleps.

For all the distance between them, she stayed in his thoughts.

In the spring of 1930, Mary persuaded Barry to send his manuscript to an editor at Little, Brown, although Barry claimed he couldn't even remember the names of the characters. Apparently it was rejected; Mary then suggested sending it to Houghton Mifflin, but Barry lost her letter with the editor's name. He asked her to send his novel to the editor with a note "asking him to do me the favor of giving me some frank criticism in view of possible future work. I am only sending the poor old war horse to him for that reason."

When the manuscript was again rejected, Barry locked it away in a trunk where it remained for the rest of his life.

He turned briefly to composing lyrics for popular songs, copyrighting one called "Baby Eyes"; set to a ukulele, the song promised, "I'll always see a heaven for me shining in baby eyes."

The Derby with its attendant houseguests and lunch-to-midnight parties took up several of Barry's May letters that year; he offered to place a bet for Mary, but she replied that she would instead spend the money on a bra.

Barry wrote, again in May 1930:

> It is really right silly, I suppose, for me to stay on in the Radio
> Department, but at least I am getting some kind of business
> training. . . . Besides, if I change now, there wouldn't be much of
> a chance of me getting a vacation this summer.

Henrietta was making plans to visit Sweden, Germany, and France,
with Edie and Barry as her companions. Barry didn't invite Mary to
join them.

Later in the spring, Barry went to Richmond for Melinda Caperton's
wedding; Mary was there as well. Afterwards he wrote that "my brains
are addled, but I can't forget the many swell details of that weekend . . .
the lovely musical-comedy wedding, and all through it your grand and
unforgettable way of looking up at me."

Before he sailed to France with Edie and Henrietta on August 13,
he sent a letter to Mary, asking her to see him off:

> Couldn't you manage to spend one night in New York and go
> back to Boston on the midnight Wednesday night? I know this
> is a violent and upsetting request when you're deep in your job,
> but I do so want us to get together in New York.
>
> You and Warren must come down, please, darling. I hope
> Warren can come too, so we can have one of those long talkative
> drinking evenings that appeal to me so strongly. Won't it be grand?
>
> Surely, after your genuine success with Little, Brown, you
> should be able to get away for a few days, so we can have another
> act of our musical comedy, with plenty of hit songs.

Six days later, he wired Mary, "So absolutely delighted you are
coming to New York. I will arrive Monday and go to the Plaza will

meet you at Grand Central barring an act of God to prevent it can't wait to see you."

After their visit, Barry wrote to her from on board the *Mauretania*,

> When I left you on the dock, I felt so miserable that I wanted to go and shut myself up somewhere in a den of roaring beasts by preference. As I staggered up the gangplank, I saw my family firmly planted nearby, and the next minute I saw the familiar swarthy face of Eduardo Andrade who is crossing on this ship. His presence has made the trip a good deal more hectic, because he insists on drinking and carrying on. . . . Eduardo and I have picked up one sallow girl from Buffalo . . . but she shies from a highball like a frightened horse.

If he wrote again during the summer of 1930, Mary didn't save his letters.

In September, Barry wired Mary, "Arriving Aquitania twenty sixth can you make New York or shall I come Boston cable Guthrie Castle." Learning that she would meet him in New York, he wired again: "Can hardly wait." After two days together—along with Edie Callahan—Mary went back to Boston and her job. Barry wired a final time, "Good night darling I love you."

This cable was the last in the collection Mary kept. Within two weeks of its arrival on October 30, 1930, Mary had made a surprising decision.

In early November her friend and benefactor, Mildred Penn, along with Zora Stephens, decided that Mary "could not go on that way" because of Barry's "bad influences and indecisive side," as Mary recalled many years later. The two women decided that she would "go to live with Zora in Paris in the sixteenth arrondissement."

There may, however, have been a last straw.

Although Mary probably never saw the letter Francis Parks wrote to Barry after his and Barry's excursion to Miami and Nassau, she certainly heard about its contents from their friend Warren Buckler. In that letter, Francis described a Boston party Mary gave for her sister Harriette,

> who is dancing here. Very amusing. The Penns, the Owens, both Whiting sisters and so on, also a philosophy professor from Harvard named Eaton who spent the evening looking Mary up and down with lechery in both his eyes. Mary asked to hear all about our trip, and I naturally began with a carefully expurgated account of the two days in Miami, but she told me rather brusquely that she had heard enough about that already and would I start with arriving in Nassau. My suspicions thoroughly aroused I waited until I saw Warren had had enough drinks to put him in a confessional mood and then found out that he . . . had entertained everybody at a party before Christmas by reading our letter. He said, "Of course I left out the part about the taxi driver soiling his britches, but Mrs. Penn read that over my shoulder." So Mary has the idea that I led you far astray in Miami. Do try to correct this impression the next time you write her.

Francis then expounded for several pages on an eighteen-year-old girl he had heard about,

> the daughter of one of the best families in these parts . . . charming and popular and plans were being made for her debut. But a few weeks ago everything was upset by the girl changing into a man. She has to shave, her voice and her nature have changed and almost overnight she developed a complete set of perfectly functioning male urino-genital organs.

He wondered how many times a day the girl's brother "puts his hand in his pocket to make sure nature isn't going about some malignant reciprocation procedure in his own anatomy? It must be a cause for considerable worry."

Francis continued:

> Does she not regret now that she maintained her virginity (of course the assumption is that she did, they do along Brattle Street) when it would have meant so little to her to have lost it and the possibilities of the dual sensations would have made her so unique. I shall look into this and let you know any further developments. It intrigues me very much.

Mary had never objected to Barry's men friends, nor did she object in light of Warren's report on Barry and Francis's adventures in Miami; from the beginning, her acceptance of his friends was as crucial to her relationship with Barry as her acceptance of his family. She may, however, with some assistance from Mildred and Zora, have felt she couldn't find satisfaction while remaining outside of the intimacy he shared with Francis, especially when faced with such overwhelming evidence of her continued exclusion.

All her life, she would fight powerfully and passionately against being left out, even when the intimacy that threatened her was between Barry and their children. But in November 1930, after nearly four years of putting up with his drinking, his immaturity, and what seemed to be the impossibility of his ever proposing, she faced an intimacy that by its nature excluded her and would continue to exclude her. That, even more than Barry's interminable stalling, may have driven her decision to move to Paris.

Strengthened by Mildred's advice and Zora's offer, Mary suddenly took matters into her own hands. In early November she wrote Barry,

"I have just cabled Zora Stephens that I would come over and spend the winter with her in Paris."

In her brief, businesslike note, she informed her "Dearest Barry" that "Life in Boston doesn't seem particularly exhilarating. I think I might as well give L. B. and Co. the air and take to my heels," abandoning the job she had worked so hard to find a little more than a year earlier.

She planned to sail immediately, on November 11, adding, "I don't know how long I will be abroad. My plans are very indefinite." She told him she might look for work in Paris in the spring.

"I feel very far away from you . . . and sad and strange."

Apparently Barry rushed to Boston; the roses he sent to Mary at the dock carried a note describing his visit to Isabella Gardner's Fenway Court and the violets under the Giorgione there. Flowers, he wrote, seemed inadequate to place before beauty, but he was trying.

His next letter, which I found in the blue box, wasn't written until November 30; he mailed it to Mary's apartment in Boston. She had given him no address in Paris.

"I don't know what to say or even to think," he wrote, "for the most numbing sense of loneliness came over me when I read your letter last night," her first letter from the ship.

He understood the appeal of a "wild time" with Zora in Paris, and expected them to "tear Montmartre limb from limb" but perhaps settle down to a quieter life in the spring. He added, "I'm so damn glad you will be with Zora, who seems to me the epitome of all that would be attractive in a companion in Paris [but] I wish I knew where you were going to live."

Two letters of the three that Mary wrote to Barry during her stormy winter crossing on the *M.S. Lafayette* are difficult to place in order, not only because they are dated only by the day of the week, but because one—typed, possibly before she left—contradicts the emotional content of the others. One was never sent.

The typed letter assumed the high, hard tone of their earlier correspondence. Mary wrote of a whirl of farewell parties in Boston, of Mildred Penn's cucumber and anchovy sandwiches—"so startlingly good I can't stop thinking about it"—and of the usual shipboard grotesques, including a woman who reminded her of the protagonist of Michael Arlen's *The Green Hat*, the same woman she believed she and Barry had seen in Venice.

As she recalled this incident from their shared past, with its slightly manufactured glamour and mystery, she seemed to be making another bid for a shared future. Her flight might be just one more step in their complicated pas de deux. But the reference to the novel sounded another note, whether intended or not.

In *The Green Hat*, published in 1923, Iris March—wearer of the hat—is a sexually liberated woman who seduces the narrator in a one-night stand. Fascinated and horrified, he tells the reader, "She was, you can see, some invention, ghastly or not, of her own. . . . I felt so profoundly incapable with her." Pregnant after their one-night stand, Iris nearly dies in a "prison" of a nursing home in Paris where apparently she is having an abortion. In the end, Iris, that "shameful, shameless lady," kills herself by driving her car into a tree.

In using her sexuality to become "an invention of her own," Iris tried to seize control of her life; in the terms of this novel, she is a monster who must be destroyed.

When she reminded Barry of this beautiful wicked heroine, Mary inadvertently pointed out the fascinated repugnance they and their friends shared for this version of the New Woman: exotic, dangerous, sexually voracious.

By leaving Boston, Mary, too, was seizing control of her own life. In the closest she came to criticism, she told Barry in her first, typed letter that she felt she wouldn't have seen anything of him that winter in Boston, because—and she understood this was appropriate—he was so engrossed in his job in Louisville that nothing else mattered. But her later handwritten letter from the *Lafayette* revealed her deep emotional turmoil. Here, she passionately regretted another letter, which she had given to Barry on their last meeting in New York in late October. She begged him to forget that letter, confessing that when he put her on the train for Boston, her pain had been so overwhelming that "I thought I would not be able to bear it any longer, and that I must try to recover myself, or at least to protect myself from such pain again." She had since realized that "what you said you were afraid of is perfectly true. I have allowed my whole emotional life to become centered on you."

Reading this letter in which she attempted so starkly to make the clean break she had for so long sought to avoid, I imagine her in one of the cheaper cabins below deck as the *Lafayette* wallowed through a storm, sitting on her bunk to write:

> You have been a pivotal influence in my life, and I have never touched yours except at the circumference and in a casual and quite quite superficial way. Our lives have been like two circles rushing through space and for a little while a very small segment of yours and mine overlapped and then rushed on without much volition or purpose . . . as haphazard as Evelyn Waugh's automobile race.
>
> And, with the dreadful persistence and willfulness and inordinate possessiveness of women in love, I have never admitted this to myself before.

She expected Barry to find this letter embarrassing and even irritating because he was, she writes, so sensitive and kindhearted, adding that all Barry's "protestations and avowals of love for me" were only "unconsciously provoked by a sense of compassion and gallantry."

In Boston her life was, she explained,

pretty drab, consisting as it did of months of a sort of suspended consciousness when the core of all my thoughts and feelings was bound up in you, and I did whatever I did in a preoccupied and sometimes distraught way, and between these times, a few days of radiant and distracting happiness when we managed to be together.

And then came their separation,

which makes me write you these long terrible letters about things I have always thought should not be written about. . . .

So now I think before this goes any further and my demands and my horrible growing possessiveness and desire humiliate me further, we had better break from it entirely. Because the present situation as you must see is intolerable for me, and there seems to be no alternative.

A few days later, still aboard ship, Mary had begun to relent. Perhaps, lacking Mildred's and Zora's support, she simply relapsed. A stormy voyage alone could have left her drowning in loneliness; this crossing was the first trip she had ever taken without family or friends. "But I do hope you won't forget me," she wrote in her next letter, "or let me get too out of touch with your life." Then she promised that she would always love him, and enclosed her Paris address, begging him to write soon.

"Thinking of you both constantly and intensely," Barry wrote reassuringly in his first letter to Mary at Zora's apartment. He then got right to the point:

Before I go one inch further on this page, I must tell you that I love you like sixteen million kinds of hell. When your letter came, the

one written on the boat, I was so cast down in the dumps I could
barely reach for the second sheet, but when I did, oh darling,
how do you know how to write just the lovely, warm, comforting
things I want to hear? Your sympathy and your understanding
surpass anything I have ever known. The things that you wrote in
your letter from the ship were so heart-breaking, my darling, and
yet I am glad you did send me that letter, along with the other. If
the first one had come alone, I would have felt lost and hopeless
and alone for good.

When she received this letter, Mary was comfortably installed in
Zora's apartment at 111 rue de Grenelle, in one of the prettiest of Paris's
Left Bank neighborhoods. She was enjoying Zora's matchmaking with,
as she later recalled, "I'm sure a counterfeit Polish count" who pursued
Mary aggressively. Beginning in Greece, Zora had made a business of
introducing Mary to eligible men, and in Paris this trend continued.

But, unbeknownst to her, Barry had suffered a far more serious
blow than any she could have given him. On December 2, 1930, he
wrote to her with his terrible news:

I came back Sunday night from Francis's funeral, longing like hell
all the way back to put my head down on your breast and tell
you how strange it made me feel. Warren says he called you, and
I suppose you can bear with me, dearest, while I pour out some
of the details.

Barry, Francis Parks, and Warren Buckler had driven to New Haven
for the 1930 Yale-Harvard game scheduled for November 25; the
three of them "got pleasantly tight, sang Harvard songs, and generally
revived the old warming collegiate feeling that is so damned nice, no
matter what anybody says." After the game, they continued to party:

It was maudlin, mad, and perfectly in the tradition we both know so well.

Suddenly, Francis and John Fox were moved to leave, and without reason they started for home. . . . All propaganda aside, Francis was not really drunk.

But then, a few miles outside of New Haven,

a car sideswiped them, turning Francis's car completely over. John was thrown out, but Francis was caught underneath it. Poor John had to run up and down the lonely road, trying to get wary motorists to stop, and he at last got Francis out.

At the New Haven hospital, doctors found that Francis had broken both arms and three ribs, but by the next day, he seemed to be out of danger. Then, the doctors "became frightened of something called gasoline poison, hastily injected a serum, and Francis's heart stopped at once." Gasoline poisoning, caused by drinking or inhaling gasoline, causes serious damage to all the organs and is fatal unless addressed immediately.

Barry's charmed circle was ruptured. He explained to Mary, "Francis was the only one of my friends who had kept relatively free of entanglements. . . . I had the feeling about him that if I ever wanted terribly to kick over the traces, he might break loose too and help me"—as he had in Miami and Nassau.

The funeral was in Francis's hometown, Westfield, Massachusetts: "It was all very unreal and terribly near the borderline of being funny in that ghastly way that things sometimes are at funerals. When they arrived at the family house at Westfield,

Up jumped a strange minister who had never known Francis and said, "Since the dear boy was so fond of poetry, I will read a selection from the Cowboy Poet," and then some unheard-of name. The poem began with a violent jerk, something about, "he was torn, mangled, from us, so suddenly." Everybody gasped. Next the old people filed by and peered in the coffin, nodding and clucking. We had the lid closed, and the eight of us dragged the incredibly heavy casket out to the tomb, where two or three old Parks lie. This was the only lovely thing about the affair. The tomb is on a hillside, under a big pine tree. It was one of those clean, pure, passionately chaste New England days in the late fall, with very white clouds blowing in a very blue sky. . . . It gave me a queer feeling of bringing Francis back to the soil from whence he had sprung, the rocky New England background that had faded almost completely in his personality.

When we got back to the house, Mrs. Parks asked to see us all. She was too fine. It seems that Francis had a letter from me in his pocket when the accident happened, and she felt a little drawn to me for that reason. She kissed me very sweetly, and began to talk about what a lovely time we all had at our Class Day, when we arranged everything and left her with nothing to do but to enjoy herself. I talked to her for a few minutes, without feeling that embarrassment that grief usually inspires.

Afterward, absorbed into a "mournful household, where a lugubrious lunch was being served," Barry noted that one relative was "acting a rather sensationally grieved role," but a young brother was being "just right. There were many relatives, mostly old, and a little boy who couldn't catch on and kept playing Yankee Doodle on a Jew's harp through the dining room."

A group of Francis's friends then drove back to Cambridge, "talking very bawdy and feeling nervous as Hell." They gathered in a Harvard room for "a raucous Irish wake," during which Barry became "violently mad at a man called Stewart Mitchell, who was supposed to have exerted a great literary influence on Francis. He began to patronize Francis in a way that just plain got me down, and I launched into an evening of denunciation" and more drinking.

Barry looked over the manuscripts crowding Francis's room, including "a voluminous diary," kept since boarding school, and some chapters of a novel called *The Fano Players*. "Two completed novels are apparently with Carl Brandt," but Francis's Nassau novel, *The Bishop's Cocktail Shaker*—"which had you and me in it, darling"—never got beyond an outline. Barry described what he found:

> The diaries are bristling with curses against Mr. Parks, and the whole situation is very ticklish in regards to the family.... Francis kept every letter he ever got, and there may be more dangerous stuff there for the family.

Even more ticklish, a single red rose was sent to the funeral from "Auntie Bennie," a name no one, not even Barry, recognized.

Barry wrote that he felt "very queer" about Francis's death, but

> somehow, not at all sad. He never had to grow out of that phase which I think of as the college phase, and I don't feel sure that Francis wouldn't have been pretty unhappy in making the necessary compromises with life.

A few days after the funeral, Warren let Barry know how Francis's parents were coping, writing,

> Mrs. Parks sits in a darkened room in the Vendome Hotel, of all places, and contemplates the purity of Francis's spirit . . . while Bunny [Francis's father] gets drunk and has orgies of weeping,

punctuated by the writing of elegiac verse. Recently, his grief took the form of seeking out the nurse who had tended Francis and running down to sleep with her, which is an odd gesture, even from a Freudian angle.

A year later, the Parkses published a handsome pale-blue memorial volume titled *Literary Fragments*, written by Francis during his college years.

Half of *Fragments* is devoted to Francis's poetry. It displays a traditional melancholy: fear of nothingness, of meaninglessness. They share the same gray emotional tone as Barry's poems, similarly published by his father in another handsome special edition. What exactly do these young men miss, or want? Enormously privileged by their good looks, their backgrounds, their education and their money—the world was their oyster, yet drinking, fast driving, and general rowdiness fell short, and even Francis's intellectual achievements, which far outshone Barry's, failed to satisfy.

Neither of them had yet developed a permanent relationship, either with a man or a woman; neither had resolved his complicated dependence on his family. A secure sense of identity seemed to elude them.

Despite his letter's preoccupation with the grotesque foolery of the funeral and its aftermath, Barry was severely shaken by Francis's death; this event marked the end of his prolonged adolescence.

After devoting pages to the funeral, he concluded, finally:

> Now I have some much more vital things to say in my awkward and blundering way. I realize that I've been a troublesome lover, dearest Mary, a very unsatisfactory one, and it may be that you have spoiled me with your unspeakably lovely sympathy and understanding. But oh my darling, don't forget me this winter. If ever you have felt that I love you, feel it a dozen times magnified now.

I have been such a damn fool on many occasions, I have had such growing pains and such flashes of a funny kind of wildness. . . . Even if you haven't always understood, you have believed in me a little, and I beg you to believe still a little more now.

Let me be explicit. I can't ask you to be true to me, because I think it is an unfair thing to demand under the circumstances. I want you to do everything and see everyone you care to, making only this plea: that you keep your heart a tiny bit open to the influence my love must generate of its own power.

I have torn this letter open to say for God's sake please don't think of our life as a thing that has been. Don't, don't, please. I am looking entirely toward the future and, God willing, we have hardly reached the beginning of a great love.

Mary had waited almost four years for this declaration.

Mary Clifford Caperton, 1924

George Barry Bingham, 1924

Coming home to Zora's apartment from a "raucous Saturday night," she found Barry's letter on the table beside her turned-down bed. She replied right away: "As I shan't be able to sleep until I have written you, I am going to, although it's terribly late . . . and I feel in that strange clairvoyant dawn-and-champagne state."

Since hearing from Warren of Francis's death, she confided,

> I have wanted so much to be with you and to give you all my love and sympathy and to share with you all the strange and unhappy reactions I have had. It was a great shock to me. I don't know quite how to say it, but it made me feel strange and alone and very sad, and as if life was perfectly incalculable and haphazard.... Darling, Darling, I am glad you wrote to me just as you did. It means so much to me, and I love you for it. I am glad you feel as you do about Francis, and glad to know everything about it because I had the deep unhappy feeling that perhaps the accident hadn't been entirely a chance one. And Francis has been a part of so much that is lovely and precious in my life that I couldn't bear for him to have that denouement.

Leaving her concerns about the cause of Francis's death unexplained, Mary continued:

> I love you and that is the only thing that matters in my life.
>
> I have felt sometimes that I was to you, in a way I can't quite understand, but only feel, a kind of responsibility that distressed and worried you, and I can't bear that. I thought about it a good deal on the boat and I wrote you a letter, which I couldn't, at the last minute, send. But I think I shall send it to you now because it explains a part at least of my whole state of mind, and I want you, just as I want you to understand and to know everything that I

do and think, to understand this rather unhappy and troubled condition of my feelings. My sweet love, I have always, as you know, been honest with you to the point of indecency, and I want you to be frank with me about this. And if you feel, in any deepest secret part of yourself, that this letter is true, or that you want this to be final, or that your love for me has changed or that the situation is irksome to you, I beg you, by everything that has ever passed between us, or everything that I may have meant to you, to tell me so.

Barry, Barry, when I read the last part of your letter again, I think that what I have written is impossible, and that I may seem to you ungenerous or stubborn. But I must write it because it is a fear that is forever tearing at my heart and making me feel desolate and far away from you. But if, with all your heart, you deny this, and if you do still love me, you must know, my darling, that there is no question of my not being true to you.

She concluded, "My darling sweet love, I do so want to come back when you can come to meet me. You do want me to, don't you?"

Barry's letter about Francis Parks' death released her for at least a moment to touch on her fears. Of all the letters she kept, Barry's response to her crucial question, and to her inclusion of her previously unsent letter, is missing.

They had reached some new level of understanding in the wake of Barry's loss. But he had not explicitly asked her to marry him, as Mary would have been keenly aware. The elaborate dance of their courtship resumed.

Only a week later, on December 9, Barry appeared to have relegated Francis's death to the past, writing Mary about going to cover a steeplechase "for the paper, and I packed some special bourbon in my suitcase against a grand and raucous party." His enjoyment of the weekend was only marred by "acute conjunctivitis, which is a polite way of saying pink eye."

His emotional resiliency had served him well during other family disasters, such as the death of his mother. Mary remembered learning—only much later—from Lizzie, Barry's maid, that seven-year-old Barry had spoken in whispers and walked on tiptoe for weeks after the car his mother was riding in was struck by a trolley. He had been sitting on her lap; she died a few days later. An ability to overlook personal sorrow, developed during his childhood, armored him for the rest of his life.

After spending Christmas with Zora at Juan-les-Pins, Mary matched his breezy tone, writing to him about

> playing baccarat at the Cannes casino and holding the bank for eight coups and then losing it all at Roulette at Monte Carlo and seeing the Aga Khan at lunch with somebody, not one of the Beguins . . . and meeting Lilian Macchiora who is half Dutch and half Irish, was born in Smyrna and had a wild affair with Constantine and who when asked to define pederasty said a pederast was a man who turned his back on women . . . et aux hommes aussi.

Perhaps fearing that all this gaiety might finally alarm her Kentucky beau, she hastened to add, "Somehow tonight I don't want to talk about it at all. I want to tell you that I love you and I miss you."

In reply, Barry wrote accommodatingly,

> How grand for you to be on the Riviera. I hope you have some swell beach pajamas that show off your figure.
> What are you doing tonight, I wonder. Maybe you are going to the Boeuf sur le Toit, or my favorite, the Grand Escart, or

to ratty old Florence's.... If I could only be with you for the evening, we might go pub crawling, and examine all the tippling palaces on both sides of the river. Even better, we might drive out the Champs Élysées, with the pink street lights shining on the wet sidewalk. I'd like most of all to kiss you right now, my darling, no matter where in hell we were. Goodnight, my Mary. I love you so much, and I'm so afraid you won't think of me.

On February 10, Barry's birthday, Mary cabled him from Paris, "Dearest I am so terribly glad you were born."

In early 1931, he was sent to Washington for two months

to be with the Washington correspondents of the Louisville papers, and learn what it is that makes Herbert Hoover that way, among other things. I will stay until Congress adjourns on the fourth of March.... All of this means that I will be in the east all ready to leap at you from the dock whenever you land, my sweet.... The important thing is that we will be together in New York, with theatres and speakeasies and night clubs and spring going on, so I'll be out of my head with joy.

But Mary, that same winter, wrote to tell him that a new friend

says she can get me a job at Jean Reigny as a mannequin. Both Schiaparelli and Patou have one American mannequin each and they have been tremendous successes. Do you think it would be amusing? Jean Reigny is the smartest house in Paris now.... Zora doesn't want me to consider it. If I could ever achieve that high-born air of swishing up and down stairs, I think it might be fun, though, just to try it for a little while.

Every evening ends with a visit to a nightclub, often Florence. Mary wrote Barry, "Florence herself is in New York, and a swell high yellow wench sings with an English accent that makes me begin to feel like the imperial mogul of the Ku Klux Klan.... I go a great deal to the Lido, a boîte where Charpini—man or woman?—does his stuff."

On January 13, 1931, Mary wrote to thank Barry for his letters and his Christmas present—a handkerchief case which Zora's maid greatly admired; she "took it and pressed it and said it must have taken beaucoup de patience to make." That Christmas, he didn't forget her: "I think it was so utterly adorable of you to send me a present, and to think of such a perfect one." The handkerchief case seems a modest tribute.

She was still uneasy about having sent him, in December, her shipboard letter, explaining again,

> I sent it to you because I can't bear to have any thoughts or feelings I can't share with you, so please, please don't think me hysterical or strange. It was the result of a mood of such despondency and loneliness that I began to doubt the reality of the most precious thing in life to me—your love, and I am sorry to have felt such things or to have doubted you.

But Barry was engrossed in his Washington, D.C., job, which included working as a police beat reporter, although he found the other reporters "a race apart." They had already "decided to try me out on the drinking question" and "since the first party they have had me half-conscious all the time. Most of the reporters are mildly drunk all the time, and they are foul-mouthed in a genuinely imaginative way" as in *The Front Page*, the Ben Hecht play he and Mary had seen together. "I've gotten fairly used to seeing 'floaters' dragged out of the river, and dead farm boys lying in pools of dried blood," but his "gorge rose yesterday" when he was sent to interview a man dying from self-inflicted burns. "My darling," he informed Mary, "he didn't have any face left."

He had also found time to act in plays at a local theatre: "The cool, musty smell of the stage, and the feel of the grease paint brought back the most vivid picture of Brattle Hall, and you getting out of the orange." (They'd first met in a 1927 undergraduate production of Carlo Gozzi's play, *The Love of Three Oranges*. Barry was the prince, Mary a fairy princess first seen stepping out of an orange.)

In a letter that Barry saved, Mary was tortured by a new anxiety. Barry had picked up a rumor, perhaps about the counterfeit "Count," which her letter declares is "not so." At last had he become jealous?

Then in February of 1931, it seems Mary caught cold. Seventy years later, she said that Zora had thought she might have tuberculosis and wanted to send her to a spa in Switzerland, but "I said that if I did have TB, I must go home and be cared for in Richmond."

She wrote to Barry with no mention of illness:

> My dearest, I have been having an awful struggle about my plans
> for coming home. Zora and Dorsey just refuse to discuss it, and
> Zora wrote Mother urging her to tell me to stay on until summer.
> Of course Mother wrote back that nothing would please her
> better, and everybody is writing and telling me not to come back.
> I am beginning to think there is a conspiracy to keep me out of
> the country.

Either Mary's decision to return home was reinforced by this opposition, especially her mother's, or else she simply chose to believe that Barry was at last ready to marry her.

Barry wrote to reassure her, "No matter where you land, I'll be planted twice life-size on the dock waiting for you," adding with his familiar equivocation, "but I hope it is when I'm still within two hours' flying distance of New York." Still, she was "surprised and joyous" when she saw him on the dock, his arms full of jonquils.

She and Barry repaired at once to the Gypsy Bar on 52nd Street, a favorite. There, over a bottle of champagne, they became engaged; the maître d'hôtel, to congratulate them, gave them another bottle. Then they called Mary's parents in Richmond. In her interview with Mary, her granddaughter Emily asked why Barry hadn't already asked Clifford, in the conventional way, for Mary's hand. Surprised, Mary replied, "Oh no, I was twenty-seven years old and taking care of myself." In that same interview, Mary remembered that the big diamond engagement ring she wore all her life was delivered the next day from Tiffany, but in fact it arrived in Richmond some weeks later.

On February 28, the day of his proposal, Barry mailed a letter to his father, written earlier from the Racquet Club in Washington. He warned him:

> This letter is going to be a very great surprise, and somewhat of a shock to you. I am about to ask Mary Caperton to marry me.
>
> Don't think that I am acting impulsively, or without proper consideration. I have known Mary for five years, and have seen her in many settings and under many varying circumstances. It is only in the last few months, however, that I have felt I am in any way ready to make a success of marriage.
>
> Circumstances have made it possible for me to consider the whole question with a little more than the usual common sense.

His letter doesn't mention Francis Parks' death. The letter continues, listing Mary's good points for his father:

> She has the most brilliant, pliant and interesting mind I have ever encountered, combined with a glorious sense of humor

and a quality that to me is more important than any other . . . an essential integrity.

"We both realize," he went on, "that we have some problems to work out, and some compromises to make" without defining in this letter what these might be.

Thanking his father for his generosity and understanding, Barry admitted, "I have been an expensive person for you and now I will be an even greater expense"—he assumed his father would be supporting the young couple, at least initially. Also, he hoped his father didn't think that he had been "intentionally secretive." Rather, Barry insisted, he had said nothing because "it is always hard for me to express myself on matters that touch me very deeply."

Barry subsequently wrote Mary in Richmond that Robert Bingham had been "a little embarrassed at first, and I discovered that he was afraid we might not like living in my cottage" a stone's throw from the Big House. But Barry reassured him on this point, and agreed readily to his father's suggestion that they take a North Cape cruise for their honeymoon, a sterner alternative to another bibulous jaunt on the Continent.

"You really mustn't be afraid of him," he instructed his not-quite-fiancée; their engagement was yet to be announced. "Never was a human being more disposed to another than he is to you." Mary knew that Robert Bingham's acceptance was crucial; as soon as she was married, she began to call him "Papa."

Barry reported that his father was "deeply touched and warmly pleased" by Mary's letter introducing herself. Robert Bingham's letter replying to hers, written on *Courier-Journal* and *Louisville Times* letterhead on March 19, 1931, congratulates her on "bringing this joy into Barry's life."

He reassured her that Barry "has never given me one moment's anxiety, or pain," intimating that he had known little about his son's drinking or had viewed it without alarm. Instead, Robert wrote:

206 • Sallie Bingham

He has brought me joy and pride, support and strength, and he has helped in many trying situations with a wisdom and judgment rare in anyone at any age.... The whole family revolves around him....

Your happiness now becomes his, and I have taken you into my heart as my very own child.

He ended with his hope that she will visit Louisville in May, when "You will see your house when the birds are singing and the flowers blooming."

In Richmond at the start of March, Mary was waiting to announce their engagement. But there were still alarms and excursions to endure before she could do so.

Exercising a new tone of authority, she wrote Barry on March 5, "I'm disappointed, my dear, about our announcement," which had been postponed because of the sudden illness of his Aunt Mary. Since Mary had not met these relatives, their health concerns seemed remote from her overriding preoccupations: to announce their engagement, set the date for their wedding, and join her sister Sarah, newly engaged, at the altar in Richmond's St. James Episcopal Church.

In that same letter, she refused Barry's suggestion to proceed despite his absence. "But my darling, to announce it without you here is perfectly untenable." Mary could not delay much longer, however, because Sarah's fiancé would "fly into a million pieces" if the joint announcement was put off again.

In an attempt to ease these difficulties, Barry's beloved Aunt Sadie had arrived from Asheville in early March; Mary remembered that she "fell in love with her at once" because of Sadie's irreverent sense of humor. Sadie made fun of Colonel Bingham—Wolfe's grim old headmaster—but always stopped short of ridiculing his son, Barry's father.

Finally Aunt Mary was out of danger, and the engagement could be announced in the Richmond, Washington, Boston, and New York newspapers, but it appeared on March 23, 1931—the week after Sarah's. The separation of the two weddings may have been a concession to the Binghams' preferences. If so, this marked Mary's first indication to her beloved older sister that new priorities were taking shape.

Now Barry wrote his soon-to-be mother-in-law, Helena, from the Racquet Club in Washington:

> It was difficult for me to believe that another drop could be added to my already brimming cup of happiness, but I found just the things that were needed for completion when I read your note. You were sweet to write me, and to make me feel that I would be welcomed into a family so filled with charming people. For years I have made my devotion to Mary an excuse for an overweening appreciation and interest in you all, and I love to think that soon I will have my own claim on you.

Perhaps he sensed Helena's uneasiness over the delayed announcement, explaining to her:

> I'm sure you understand my impatience to have our engagement announced. It is such a matter of pride to me that I want all the telephone operators and cab drivers and colored doormen to know about it, and besides, it is another needed assurance of the reality of the whole situation.

Back in Richmond, Sarah's engagement to her fiancé had been announced in the New York papers on March 15, but there would be no plans for a joint wedding. Sarah's would take place the following month; Mary's a little later, in early June. As preparations for Sarah's wedding proceeded, the atmosphere at 1510 West Avenue was more than usually chaotic. Mary wrote Barry that Helena was working all morning hammering out a long Old Virginia Never Tire account of the beauties of Virginian colonial houses with the wet wallpaper which the colored men were snatching from the walls literally streaming down the back of her neck.

Someone was going to have to pay for the family's two weddings and Helena was doing her part, cranking out the kind of article the local newspapers might buy.

Mary added:

> I have been away from this family vortex for so many years that it seems quite odd and strange to be suddenly thrown into this violent intimacy and is all the more sort of obliquely funny because they are completely unaware of how strongly they affect my appreciative faculties.

Disappointed that Barry didn't attend Sarah's April wedding, Mary described it for him:

> Sarah looked perfectly adorable and said "I will" in a clarion stern voice quite out of order. And when Harriette was unpinning her veil to uncover her face she stuck the pins in her (H's) mouth in the most unconcerned way in the world, just like Minnie Scott [the seamstress] goes fitting you tight around the fanny.

She filled him in on all the family's festivities, writing that "Tonight [April 21] Harriette is going to dance at the Beaux Arts Ball. She is to enter the Jefferson Hotel lobby on a white horse, dismount and flit about."

After all the hubbub, at last Mary traveled to Louisville in May to visit the two Bingham family houses where she would spend the rest of her life. If she wrote about her impressions, she didn't put the letter in the blue box. But in her oral account, she admitted that Robert Bingham's Big House "looked awfully grand to someone reared in near poverty as I was." Barry's bachelor villa, the "Little House" across the lawn, was slightly less imposing.

After Mary returned to Richmond, Barry wrote:

> My own Darling, I am so lonely for you that I can't make sense.... I feel all hollow inside, and the next three weeks seem as endless a period as the three weeks before Christmas when we were children. The popular songs, my darling, have handed us a lot about walking around in a dream and all that, and as usual there is a strong element of truth in the peculiar hit song philosophy. The days you were here seem so unreal now that I am half afraid they never happened at all. Did we really have breakfast together, and watch Twenty Grand run together, and particularly, did we really go swimming in the starlight, and lie along the grass so close together? Surely, my dearest, that was too beautiful to have been a part of anybody's life that is generally so filled with eating and sleeping and sitting in an office. You were so beautiful that I can't believe anything could be so elusively and aesthetically lovely and yet so warm and dear there in my arms. I have always loved those dark nights when the stars give such a faint and secret light and now I shall always think of the cool splash of the water, and the feel of the dewy grass, and the clean beauty of your body shining strangely in the shadows.

As for visiting Richmond, Barry wrote, "It hardly seems, as far as I can see, that there is the possibility of our having to effect another delay." But his Aunt Mary suffered a relapse, "spoiling our possibilities for this weekend." Barry described his aunt as "brilliant and majestic, with a wit that was sharp and devastating. She was never what could have been called a sympathetic person."

As an example of her influence, Barry wrote Mary that when he was being forcibly toilet-trained as an infant, he would "have strong crying spells about going to the bathroom" because of his fears of the swirling water when the toilet was flushed. When Aunt Mary was called in, "I immediately performed without further protest," which explained her impact on the engagement announcement.

Receiving a letter from Barry "while Mother and I were seated over a late breakfast of great mounds of batter bread and roe herring," Mary was so pleased by the news that his Aunt Mary was better that "I could hardly go on raising my fork to my mouth." She sent to Barry her fondest hopes that his aunt would continue with her recuperation:

> I wish Aunt Mary would live.... I can't bear to have anyone leave this perfectly grand world, and particularly anyone who loves you and knew you when you were afraid of the johnny seat. I know so well how you felt that it nearly drives me crazy. I always thought Odysseus must have had just the same feeling about Charybdis. I know it's not spelled that way. But do lets have a real quiet, stealthy one in our nursery bathroom.

Mary reassured Barry, "Of course Mother and Artown [Sallie] are delighted and Father did not fall into a swoon." She closed her letter by assuring Barry that she loved him "with all my heart, with all my mind, and with all my soul, like my duty to my God." Her effusive vow held the seeds of inevitable disappointment; as a woman who considered herself "not religious," she may already have been disillusioned with God, but even that disappointment might pale compared to disillusionment with her husband. She tried to explain her feelings to Barry, and also to herself:

It is strange, love, that my feeling of preoccupation and absorption in you make me more keenly alive and aware of everything else in the world and not, as it is supposed to do, amazed or mazed, in Mr. Kittredge's sense of the word—so that what casual people say even, or noises in the street, and the idiosyncrasies of speech strike me sharply and intensely and I feel always a secret and keen and sweet delight in these things that seem to me almost unbearably lovely or pitiful or enchanted. It seems to me that all my powers of perception are refined and sharpened and as if my consciousness were something like a trim and vibrant and brittle piece of blown glass washed about by waves of light and color and sound.

In preparation for the delayed engagement announcement, Barry finally informed his North Carolina relatives of his nuptial plans, somewhat to their bewilderment since he hadn't mentioned Mary before. Aunt Sadie asked her famous question, "Is she a Democrat and an Episcopalian?" and received the satisfactory answer.

As the news of their engagement spread, Mildred Penn cabled, "Overjoyed your news.... Cannot plan now. Congratulate Barry." She did not come to the wedding, although she did mail a check.

In May, after her visit to Louisville, Mary's letters began to lay out plans for their married life. She hoped they would never treat their love

with that curious contemptuous and almost bitter irreverence that some married people seem to enjoy displaying.... And, darling, we shall always be kind and gentle and polite to each other and kiss each other good-morning, and knock on the bathroom door, and if we are ever cross, we will never, never use our love to wound or distress one another, will we, my own darling?

There were to be no scenes like the ones that rocked the Caperton household.

Mostly, though, Mary's letters were love and more love—with bursts of practicality. After showering Barry with promises of undying love—"To you and to you alone, throughout all time and eternity, I can show my secret heart, to you and to you only"—she suggested that, in their exchange of vows, "troth" should be pronounced to rhyme with "loath," and helpfully included suggestions about how tactfully to indicate this to the clergyman.

Sarah was already married and Mary was swiftly becoming a Bingham, but there were still occasions when the two sisters got together. Mary reported to Barry that she and Sarah

> drove out to the club and sat drinking great glasses of iced orange juice and looking out over the valley full of trees all veiled in lavender mist with the cool green sky going down to the horizon in a gold sunset. Your father's birds were making noises and a remote and blessed stillness came over me when I thought that every spring after this one would be ours together and that our life would be something like that afternoon with a background of profound peace and fulfillment.

For the first time in her letters to Barry, she hinted at the virtues of drinking juice rather than liquor, explaining, "I like tomato juice rather thin and very cold with lots of seeds and an occasional piece of tomato in it and lots of lemon juice, don't you?"

She was touched by the warm supportive letters she was receiving from friends, but hoped "our first tomato red baby won't be afflicted with all sorts of odd sweaters and booties from all the strange people who have yearned over us for so long," waiting patiently for their marriage.

Barry was still in Louisville—and so the quantities of letters—although Mary longed for him to curl his fingers around a cold glass (of tomato juice?) and to "suffer your agoraphobia with me." The tumult at West Avenue might have been more than Barry could face.

He was missed at the Richmond parties honoring the couple in the run-up to their wedding. He wrote to Mary with hopes that she was enjoying them, but with no apologies: "Are you all keyed up with corn liquor and lack of sleep to that pitch which makes everything clear-cut at the edges?" In response, she pleaded, "When you possibly can, at the very first moment, will you come, my love?"

Neither Barry's brother Robert nor his sister Henrietta planned to attend the wedding. Henrietta's prospective absence bothered Barry, who wrote to Mary that "I'm disappointed, and it doesn't seem at all right for her not to be at our wedding," but it was useless to urge Henrietta. He had no idea why she would not attend, since "she gives no hint of her reasons for staying in London." But then Henrietta decided to come after all, prompting Mary to write a sentence reminiscent of her mother's best, saying she was looking forward to seeing "those purple eyes and tangled lashes."

It was becoming clear that Helena and Clifford could not afford the sort of wedding the Binghams expected, and discreet arrangements were made. Barry's father would give the couple their flat silver, traditionally presented by the parents of the bride; Barry's stepmother, Aileen, wanted a crest, but Mary campaigned for a less ostentatious shell pattern—and won. Aileen also gave the silver service: a teakettle, sugar, creamer, and other tea tray ornaments; Mary objected that Aileen was being too generous. The bride-to-be cancelled an order for silver corn holders because, she explained to Barry, she liked to eat as much of her food as she could with her hands.

Other wedding presents flooded in to 1510 West Avenue, two hundred and twenty-six in all, each meticulously noted by Helena or

Mary in a once-ivory satin book called "Gifts and Givers," also stored in the blue box. The calling cards that came with the presents were carefully numbered; Mary, writing on her new Tiffany-blue letter paper with her married name at the top, acknowledged each gift.

There were silver cigarette trays and lighters, liquor sets, silver and glass pickle stands, wine coolers, fish knives, a ruby glass decanter—but also a complete set of Charlotte Brontë's works, a fine copy of *Don Quixote* and one of *The Canterbury Tales*. The note with *Don Quixote* reads, "Hoping that the dear old Don, dusty and shabby as he is, may find an inch or two of resting space on your hospitable bookshelves." Mary noted in the satin-bound register that it was "A beautiful copy," one which she kept for the rest of her life.

Louise Burleigh sent a pair of swan almond holders. The Gulicks gave the couple an embroidered table cover, and various Lefroy relatives mailed checks. Warren Buckler presented them with a pair of silver salad forks. He, and Barry's other groomsmen, had their names engraved on a silver martini shaker. It's two feet tall.

Tellingly, there was neither telegram nor wedding present from Zora Stephens. Neither Mildred Penn nor Zora Stephens attended the wedding, absences which signaled the departure of Mary's closest friends.

Warren Buckler made plans to come to Richmond by train. Mary noted that she disapproved "mightily of Warren's coming down in the same compartment with Hattie [her sister Harriette]. She may name him as a co-respondent." Since Harriette was not yet married, the risk could not have been great.

Miss Jenny, Mary's Richmond teacher, gave a copy of James Branch Cabell's *Between Dawn and Sunrise*. She had already congratulated Mary at an Old Girls' Tea for graduates of St. Catherine's; her endorsement meant a great deal.

The date of Mary and Barry's wedding was set for June 9. Mary mailed invitations from Barry's guest list, all "in beautiful order"; he wished he could help her address the envelopes but added that they'd probably spend a half hour discussing each personality, considerably slowing the process. He was self-conscious about the large number of names he'd sent her, observing that some of these friends would nearly die of shock when they heard that he was to be married.

"Darling, do you want church invitations sent to the servants?" Mary asked in a postscript. They had given a tray as a wedding present, she reminded him, explaining that, "Lizzie and Minnie and Louise Hawkins always got [invitations to the Caperton weddings]. If you do, I think your Lizzie and Ophie ought to have them too."

Barry's stepmother, Aileen, also put together an impressive list. Eighteen Louisvillians would arrive by train for the ceremony and Mary was busy reserving hotel rooms.

In Louisville Barry was also going to celebratory parties but found time to mail Mary Henry Fielding's *Tom Jones* and Daniel Defoe's *Moll Flanders*; she joked that the two spent the night together on the train to Richmond.

Minnie Scott, the Caperton family's seamstress, was "permanently employed" making underwear for Mary's trousseau, as well as the monogrammed satin panels she would use to cover her underwear when she left it on hotel room chairs. Minnie also made Mary's going-away suit, a rather odd rabbit print (Mary mailed Barry a swatch, also preserved in the blue box) with white collars and cuffs. Mary ordered a pair of white riding breeches and a hunting jacket, preparing to learn to fox hunt in Kentucky.

Mary's sisters were to be her bridesmaids. They were to wear pastel organdy dresses; decades later, she worried that this sounded "tacky" to the granddaughter who was interviewing her.

Barry planned to bring a portable phonograph to play records on their train ride through the Virginia and Pennsylvania mountains at the start of their honeymoon. He featured a Gershwin tune called "Delilah Was a Floozie." Mary suggested adding her favorite, Irving Berlin's "Someday I'll Find You."

Amid all the planning, Mary wrote Barry that Helena would not be able to afford to serve bourbon at the wedding reception, and corn liquor was simply out of the question; there would only be champagne, and that in limited quantities. (Mary's sister Helena reported later, however, "a pint of Old Forester was put in each hotel room every day." This may have been wishful thinking since Prohibition was not repealed until 1933.)

In May, first Barry and then Mary spent ten days at Tennessee's Tate Springs Hotel, a spa where they planned to "taper off" their drinking with pitchers of mineral water. Someone had lowered the boom, perhaps Robert Bingham or the resolute Helena.

Something else alluded to in their correspondence happened at Tate Springs during the time when their visits overlapped. Mary called their brief meeting at Tate Springs in a letter as "a beautiful and moving prelude" to

> a perfect and fitting and incredibly beautiful expression—or fulfillment. I do want it so much, my own love. . . . I can hardly bear to put these things into words, my precious love, for fear of injuring in some way a perfection of feeling and expression that seems to me as delicate and fresh and innocently lovely as flowers are in a garden on a dewy morning.

Remembering the wedding many years later, Mary's sister Helena wrote, "We had a special car on the C&O Railway [from Louisville to Richmond]. It was hot as hell" which had not deterred her husband from bringing along his "moulting" fighting cocks, and the birds were moulting. They had hired a place outside of Richmond to hold a cock fight and the idea was Kentucky versus Virginia.... Cockfights were illegal in both states at that time and the birds wore steel spurs and were pitted against each other until one died.... Virginia, sadly to say, beat us.... My husband had to cover all the bets laid by Barry's groomsmen since they were right out of college and didn't have the money to settle up.

Helena added that she didn't go—"I hate the idea of cock fighting— but it was a real party and Mother didn't object as she was in favor of anything resembling a party."

Finally the wedding took place June 9, 1931, at the church where each of Mary's sisters had been married: St. James Episcopal Church in Richmond, Virginia. The wedding photograph displays the anonymous symmetry such occasions seem to create; faces are indistinct, long dresses and cutaways dominate, with a hint of garden flowers in the background.

In a portrait of the bride and groom alone, more details emerge. Mary wears a transparent muslin cap over her marcelled blond waves; a huge veil descends from the cap, merging with her forward-swept train; she looks as though she is standing in a sea of foam. At her side Barry, correct and incredibly young in his striped morning trousers and dark cutaway, looks down at her with cool affection. Her delicate, uptilted profile is serene yet slightly hesitant. Their smiles are muted, formal. There is no hint of the complexities that have brought them finally to this patch of lawn in front of pine trees and a large white house.

Barry wrote his father a celebratory note: "My deepest love and gratitude come to you on the happiest day of my life."

They spent the first few nights of their honeymoon at an inn in Albemarle County, then traveled on to Nantucket for a "not very comfortable" stay at the White Elephant, as Mary remembered it, although Barry described the place in his letters home as "this delightful Nantucket cottage."

Mary mailed a letter to her mother at 7 p.m. the day after the wedding. Her letter itself has been lost, but a page Barry had added to it remains in the blue box:

> I must put my oar in to tell you how utterly and absorbingly happy I am, and what grand fun we are having being married....
> Is it quite correct for the groom to have enjoyed the actual wedding ceremony and the grand reception more than anything that ever happened?

In July, they embarked on a North Cape cruise, per Robert Bingham's earlier suggestion, in a small steamship that sailed around Iceland and Norway. It was so cold that when sitting on deck to see the midnight sun, Barry and Mary fortified themselves with a bottle of sherry.

Later, in London, they met up with Barry's father and stepmother and began a round of parties; Robert would be appointed American ambassador to the Court of St. James two years later, in 1933, and his contacts in Scotland and England were already extensive.

One day, as the two couples were being driven down the Strand in London, their chauffeur announced, "Sir, that car ahead of us belongs to Mrs. Simpson, and she is in it!"

On another day, Robert took his newest daughter-in-law to "Cartier's where he bought me those terrific diamond and sapphire clips that make a pin," Mary recalled. "He said, 'I'm going to give you this and it gives me great joy. But I would rather that you didn't say anything to Aileen,'" Barry's stepmother and Robert's third wife. Later, when Mary wore the pin, Aileen "took one look and asked what dress it had come on?" It was the beginning of years of silent enmity.

Then Mary and Barry were off to Paris, where they met Henrietta and a British officer who, as Mary remembered, started a fight in a bar by threatening to "flatten the bugger" who'd made a homosexual insinuation. A family legend has the man buying a diamond necklace for Henrietta and charging it to Barry's hotel bill.

Leaving Henrietta and her impulsive friend behind, Mary and Barry proceeded to Venice where they bought Italian furniture for Barry's Louisville villa. There they ended their honeymoon. From Italy, they returned to Louisville, the city where they would spend the rest of their lives.

Five years later, in February of 1936, Barry paid off the mortgage on Helena's house at 1510 West Avenue in Richmond. His check, for 5,670 dollars, would be the first of many.

Mary's prediction of a basket full of tomato-red babies came true: Worth and Barry were born in quick succession, followed by me, Jonathon, and Eleanor.

Mary's position as Barry's chief confidant and intimate was severely challenged when he enlisted in World War II in 1941; he was stationed in London and the Pacific for the ensuing four years, with only one furlough home.

His frequent letters did not quiet her fear that she was losing him, a fear I glimpsed when I saw the photos he sent home, resplendent in his naval uniform at a multitude of parties. One startling snapshot from his tour of duty in Guam revealed a group of naked men in a jungle pool.

I came close, even as a seven-year-old, to understanding my mother's jealousy when I saw a snapshot of my father at Christmastime, beaming at a British girl my age, surrounded by Christmas presents.

Driven to desperation by his absence and her loneliness, Mary traveled to Washington in 1942 to apply for a pass so that she could join Barry in London, explaining that she would write newspaper articles about the effect of the war on women. A bureaucrat turned her down coldly, telling her to go home and take care of her small children. At that, Mary admitted in her oral history, "I lost my mind."

Since my older brothers would soon be sent away to boarding school and my younger brother and sister were not yet born, I was the only small child at home. Mary's fury turned on me: a sensitive, moody five-year-old who missed her father. As Mary saw it, I prevented her from going to London to be with her husband and stave off whatever threats to their marriage she saw or imagined there.

Once she regained her sanity a few months later, she found a way, true to her character, to make it up to me: by writing down poems I dictated to her after my naps. Barry, perhaps sensing how important this expression was to me, sent from London a red leather, gilt-edged journal, embossed with my name in gold letters. Mary copied my poems into this beautiful book, correcting and improving until they were, in some sense, no longer mine. Eventually she sent the book back to Barry, once more invoking the power of words to both repair and deceive.

In 1945, when Barry returned from overseas, he was restored to Mary, who was thus reassured.

•

I continued to write as a child, teenager, and young adult. In 1957, when I was—as she had been so many years before—a junior at Radcliffe, I would be surprised by the attention stirred up by a short story of mine, "Winter Term." A story of the sexual relationship between a Harvard boy and a Radcliffe girl, it was published in the *Harvard Advocate* and received the Dana Reed Award for fiction by an undergraduate—the first time the award was won by a woman. Subsequently, *Mademoiselle* acquired the piece, and it won me a coveted guest editorship.

I had, by that time, stopped showing my short stories to my parents. Much as I enjoyed their attention, I had realized that there were topics, and points of view, which I wanted to address that they would never endorse. I was sailing off into that vast sea that is the changing world around us.

I had not known how embroiled my mother had been in the controversy that swirled around "Winter Term." Sex was hardly an unusual subject even in the closely supervised 1950s. Mary's role came to light when I found, again in the blue box, carefully preserved copies of the exchange she'd had about "Winter Term" with Radcliffe Dean Mildred Sherman.

As Mary was a member of Radcliffe's Public Relations committee, she began by registering her dismay at the widespread reaction to the short story "A Sentimental Education," written by a 1952 Harvard graduate, Harold Brodkey, and recently published in *The New Yorker.*

Mary outlined her reaction for the dean:

> When I read it, I was distressed by the circumstantial and graphic description of the ways and means by which a pretty sordid Harvard-Radcliffe affair was carried on.... I tried to rebuke myself for such a Mrs. Grundy reception of what was, really, a very well-executed piece of realistic writing. But my distress on the score of Radcliffe's public relations has deepened considerably since the magazine *Mademoiselle* has bought Sallie's Dana Reed Award story and plans to publish it in the autumn. As you probably know, this story is on the same theme.
>
> I am in a very odd position in this matter, as I am enormously proud of the distinction Sallie achieved in winning the award and enormously repelled by the achievement that won it.

By the time of her writing, she and Barry had already commiserated with my tutor, Monroe Engel; Mary wrote that after reading my story, all three "felt ill for days." I was unaware of this attack of group indigestion.

Mary went on to explain that she knew that "gossip and canards about the loose sexual behavior of women in all the institutions is routine," yet she hated to add fuel to the fire, while distrusting her own objectivity in the matter "because of my involvement with the author of 'Winter Term.'" She recognized that works of the imagination—even if they sounded realistic—were secure from censorship because of "the great Harvard-Radcliffe liberal tradition." The only remedy she suggested was tightening the college parietal rules.

A few days later, the dean replied that the two stories had indeed been brought up at the public relations meeting. Sherman wrote that, in her opinion,

> "Winter Term" is a much better story than Brodkey's, but it is even more brutal, and although it does not name Radcliffe and Harvard, there can be no doubt in anyone's mind as to which institutions these two characters are attending.

While Dean Sherman and her counterpart at Harvard had agreed to maintain "a dignified silence" about the Brodkey story, the news that mine was to be published in *Mademoiselle* spurred her to action: "I telephoned Cyrilly Abels, Managing Editor of *Mademoiselle*, and a Radcliffe student of the class of 1926, and discussed with her Radcliffe's situation." Abels expressed to the dean her opinion "that only those of us who are close to the situation would really be at all disturbed by the nature of the story which she has every intention of printing."

This tempest seems to have died down after the dean's final note to Mary, reminding her that *Peyton Place* was at the time a bestseller—

an argument that would have had little resonance for Mary—and therefore "sordid" themes had entered the literary mainstream.

It was already polluted. While D. H. Lawrence's novel, *Lady Chatterly's Lover,* would only be released from its U. S. ban in 1959, James Joyce's *Ulysses* had received its reprieve in 1933.

But, in 1958, the year after this hushed contretemps, the editor of *Harper's Bazaar* canceled publication of Truman Capote's *Breakfast at Tiffany's* because of corporate pressure over the story's contents. A year later John Updike's *Rabbit, Run* caused protest by the lawyers at Alfred A. Knopf because its plot included adultery. Knopf urged Updike to cut the offending passages and, fearing that his publisher would drop the novel, Updike complied.

So Dean Sherman was in good company when she wrote to my mother seeking permission to ask me to make changes in the story, permission that Mary readily granted. The dean hoped that I would not be identified as a Radcliffe student in the magazine's biographical note, but of course I was.

Mary also informed the dean:

> I have not said anything to Sallie about our exchanges on this subject. She knows that we disapprove of the story on grounds of taste, and found it extremely unappetizing.... I do not want her to think we are persecuting her, and, as her relationship to us about her writing is extremely close (she always brings her new stories to us to be read, and listens, with rare patience, to our criticisms) I do not want to do anything that would upset that equilibrium.

She hadn't noticed that I had stopped showing my writing to my parents the previous summer.

Years later, Mary told her granddaughter that she had also feared that, because of the story, I would "get myself pregnant."

In the end, though, "Winter Term" may have offended Mary not because of its mild sexual explicitness but because of its portrait of a woman obsessed with an elusive man, who struggles strenuously, and fruitlessly, to escape. For Mary, who had waited so long, and given up so much to catch Barry, the idea that such persistent love might be an obsession hateful to its object would have been unbearable.

After my visit with the dean over "Winter Term"—which aroused a great deal of shame in me—I cut place names from the story. She had convinced me that otherwise Radcliffe's fundraising would be decreased. I had no wish to cause the college difficulties. But this was the last time I censored my writing.

Mary's consternation was soothed by the awards I won: the Dana Reed Award, and the Phi Beta Kappa Prize two years running for "the best original or creative work." My other award-winning stories from those years, "The Birthday of the Infanta" and "A Matter of Principal," have disappeared, but "Winter Term" lives on in various anthologies, its shocking intimations long since upstaged.

As her dismay subsided in the years after I graduated from college, Mary began to introduce me to important critics and writers, just as she had done for Helena in the 1940s. A 1967 letter from Katherine Anne Porter attests to her successful introduction: "I shall be happy to see your daughter Sallie's first collection of short stories." Porter explained further:

> I already know a story of Sallie Bingham's. . . . I was reading
> my copy of the Harvard book—I can't remember the title—a
> splendid anthology of writings by former students: and one
> of the newer stories that struck me was a really brilliant—and

really sad—story of the fearful kind of trap the young fall into in their first blinded steps into that dark forest. It was a very young story, too, taking its first steps, but I was impressed by it, and noted the writer's name. . . . But I did not, of course, connect her with your household.

Porter wrote a fine endorsement on the jacket of my very first book.

AFTERWORD

A few years ago, on a warm fall evening, I was sitting on the top tier of the ruins at Delphi in Greece. I hadn't yet read Mary's letter in the blue box describing that spot eighty years earlier. I did not hear the donkey bells or the wrangling of "peasant women" that had scored the pellucid air during my mother's visit, but I was blissfully alone, as she had been, although she was missing the man who would become my father.

In that place, it occurred to me that her greatest gift to me was a passion for writing.

Three generations of women writers have come before me: Sallie in letters and essays, Helena in short stories and essays, and Mary in letters and essays on education. All three women used writing as a way to temper their experiences of the world, and perhaps even to influence it, when such influence was not otherwise permitted.

They each had their methods and their measures of determination. Sallie was adept at smoothing over rough passages in a difficult life. Helena turned to articles and stories to earn a living when her husband's income fell short. Mary used her letters to persuade a man to marry her and to hone her great descriptive skills.

Despite their efforts, the world chugged along around them, often in brutal contrast to the records they kept. The Civil War surrounded Sallie with bloody battles and immeasurable violence, and her family's adherence to outmoded traditions left her no independent path to navigate through the changes the War brought, except for the Richmond Woman's Club. During Helena's era, girls were virtually sold into marriage for economic gain and had no clear recourse if their marriages did not provide for them. Helena's house on West Avenue was loud with strife, and the five daughters she herded into marriages suffered a variety of ills, chiefly the effects of alcoholism and the same corroding disappointment their mother had endured. Of all her daughters, Mary had the fairy-tale marriage that lasted, but the scholarship she had pursued so zealously, with its prospect of a wider life, led only to a conventional domesticity.

For all three women, the ideas and prejudices of their times worked powerfully on their characters and their behavior. For Sallie, the pervasive myth of an inherent racial and class hierarchy distorted her observations of life in Richmond before and after the Civil War. In Helena's case, her native talent as a writer was cramped by her need to set down the romantic tales and humorous domestic essays she knew would sell. For Mary, the prestige and security of money and social power encouraged her increasingly indefensible faith in the absolute right of the privileged and educated to rule.

Sallie, Helena, and Mary supported and were in turn supported by their allegiance to the patriarchy in all its rigid, romanticized Southern guises: a code of chivalry, a disingenuous nostalgia for plantation life, the prestige of the Richmond German and its debutantes, and the necessary and inevitable subservience of people who would always, in their minds, be first and foremost slaves or the descendants of slaves. This patriarchy also endorsed a certain kind of education, founded on the Greeks and a gentleman's library of books. This, too, was these women's inheritance.

Sallie benefited from John Henry Montague's love of books; as his adored oldest daughter, she never questioned his faith in the King James Bible, nineteenth-century British Romantics, and Victorian and Edwardian poetry. Helena drank from the same well, though she tasted a little more wildness in Ireland. Mary seemed as a teenager to look for other influences—Louise Burleigh might have begun to open doors before her own conversion to racism. But the education Mary received at St. Catherine's and at Radcliffe drew almost exclusively from the literary wells she shared with her mother and grandmother. And, by the time of Mary's marriage, even Louise Burleigh had succumbed to society's considerable pressure to conform.

These women are long dead, and their youngest descendants have never known them or, in some cases, even heard of them. The world we live in has changed so much from their time that their histories serve in many ways as monuments to what we have gladly lost.

But in addition to the prejudices we can no longer afford, we have lost, as writers and as readers, the rich yet precise language Sallie, Helena, and Mary wielded to such effect. In losing the roots of our language, as well as our family and culture, we have deprived ourselves of a grand, if ambivalent, tradition.

"What is the woot?" Helena as a little girl would ask.

Her faith in the roots, which sustained her in an often-difficult life, created her sense of rectitude, the indomitability that straightened her spine and underscored her opinions. "Vanity of vanities, all is vanity," she would quote from Ecclesiastes when facing intolerable situations.

For Sallie, who braved hardships with élan, her sense of rectitude and her resulting indomitability were also linked. She would never have allowed herself to say aloud, with Tennyson's Mariana, "I am aweary, aweary / Oh God, that I were dead."

Mary, in a far more complex time, forged the link explicitly between language and lineage, facing tragedy with Virgil's recognition of the eternal "tears in things."

The world we live in today does not lend itself to these certainties, or to the sense of rectitude they create and reinforce. We live in complexity and must discover the nuanced language that can perhaps express it. We cannot afford a well-developed sense of rectitude, or the faith in our superiority, as individuals or as a culture, that sustains it. A straight spine, now, seems to invite breaking.

My words are not the words my righteous foremothers used. Instead, as Adrienne Rich wrote, "the thing I came for: / the wreck and not the story of the wreck / the thing itself and not the myth."

But how will I ever know I'm right?

ACKNOWLEDGMENTS

Eleanor Bingham Miller, for the loan of the blue box and its contents.

Emily Bingham, for permission to quote from her interview with her grandmother, Mary Caperton Bingham.

The Filson Historical Society, Louisville, Kentucky, for permission to quote from the papers of Mary Caperton Bingham and George Barry Bingham.

The James Branch Cabell Library of Virginia Commonwealth University, Richmond, Virginia, for permission to quote from the papers of Helena Lefroy Caperton.

Helena Sliney for permission to quote from her memoir of her great-grandmother, Helena Lefroy Caperton.

Susan Hazen Hammond

Born and raised to write, Sallie Bingham published her first novel two years after graduating from Radcliffe College, followed by two collections of short stories. After taking time off to raise three sons, she published a memoir, four novels, and three more collections of short stories. She is the author of nearly a dozen plays, some of which have been produced in off-Broadway and regional theatres. She is also the founder of The Women's Project in New York, The Kentucky Foundation for Women in Louisville, Kentucky, and the Sallie Bingham Archive of Women's History and Culture at Duke University in Durham. Bingham is currently working on a biography of Doris Duke, forthcoming from Farrar, Straus & Giroux (2015).

Sarabande Books thanks you for the purchase of this book; we do hope you enjoy it! Founded in 1994 as an independent, nonprofit, literary press, Sarabande publishes poetry, short fiction, and literary nonfiction—genres increasingly neglected by commercial publishers. We are committed to producing beautiful, lasting editions that honor exceptional writing, and to keeping those books in print. If you're interested in further reading, take a moment to browse our website at sarabandebooks.org. There you'll find information about other titles; opportunities to contribute to the Sarabande mission; and an abundance of supporting materials including audio, video, a lively blog, and our Sarabande in Education program.